101 Things
- to do with a -
Dead Body

by Jason Blake
&
Emily Caesar

Copyright © 2018 by Jason Blake

All rights reserved. This book or any portion thereof may not be reproduced or used in any manner whatsoever without the express written permission of the publisher except for the use of brief quotations in a book review.

Printed in the United States of America

First Printing, 2010

ISBN : 978099771163

Laki Press
2110 Kaneka St. #160
Lihue HI 96766

"For the silly people..."

1.

foot stool.

2.

A place to store loose change.

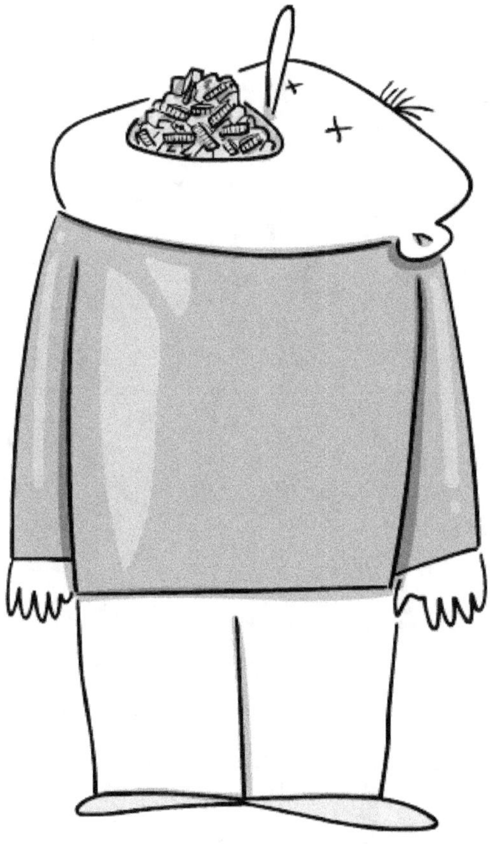

3.

Mall security.

4.

Crash test dummy.

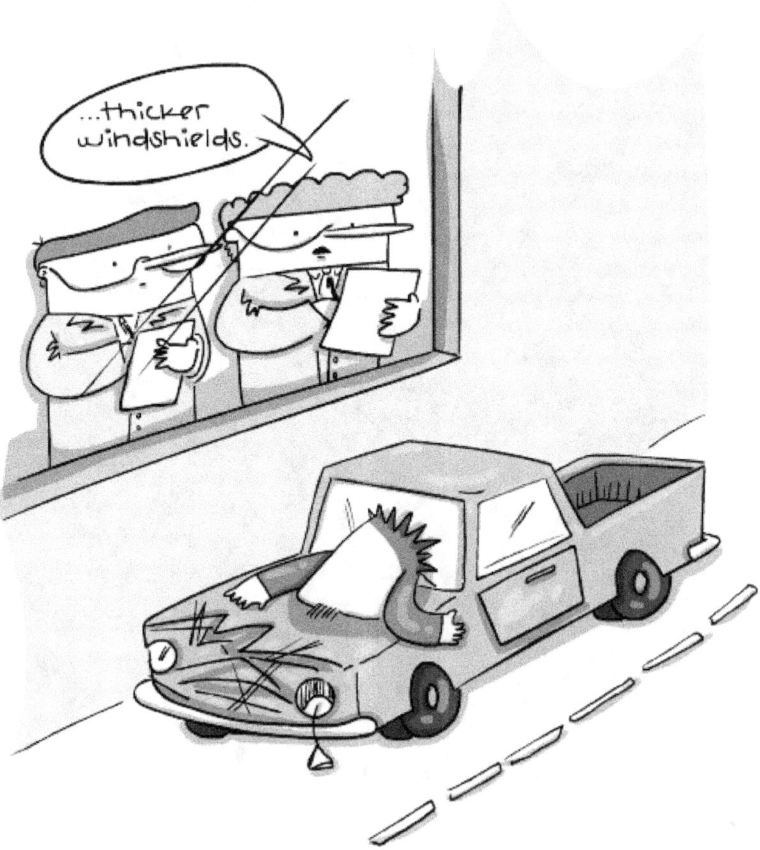
...thicker windshields.

5.

your Garden gnome.

6.

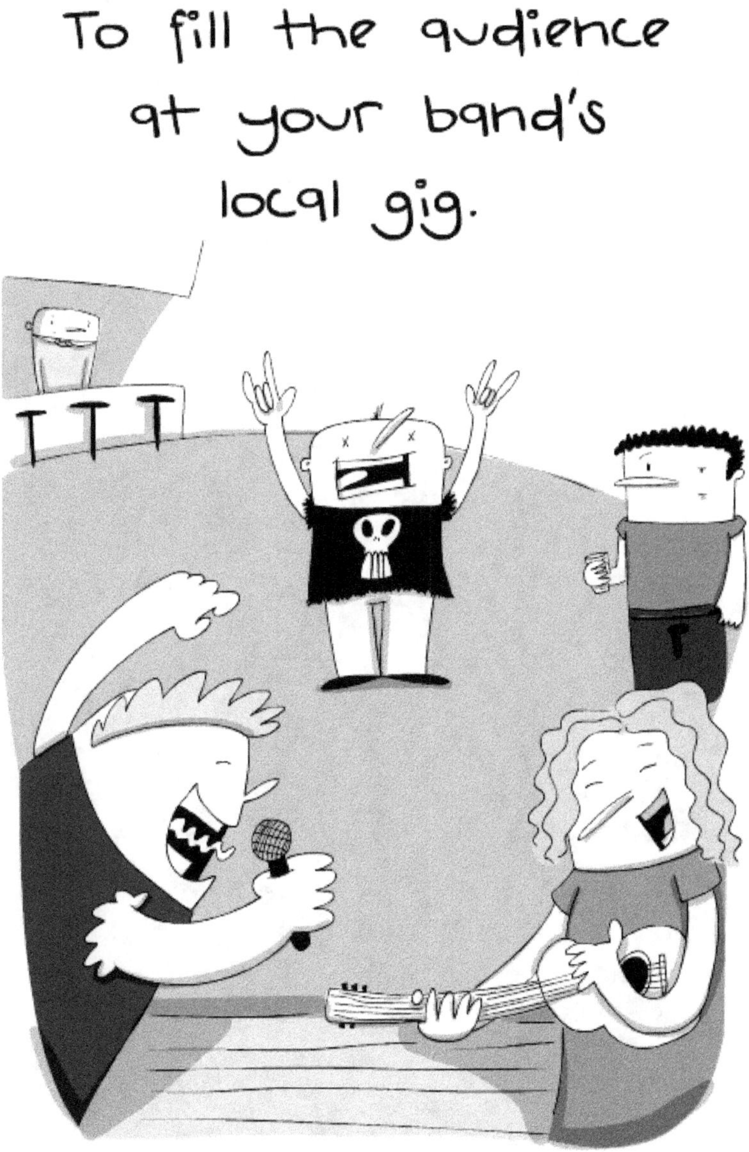
To fill the audience at your band's local gig.

7.

To fill potholes because the county won't get around to it.

8.

For CPR training.

Keep up the chest compressions.

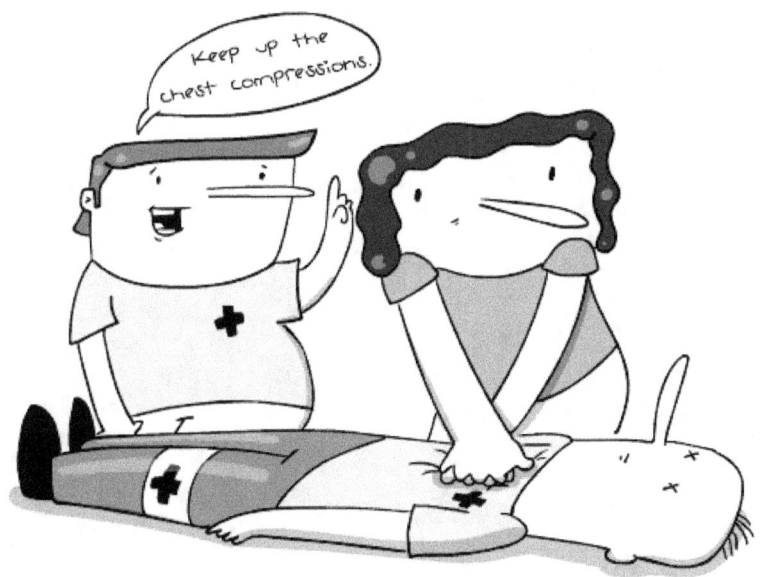

9.

A surfboard.

10.

Window clerk at county permitting office.

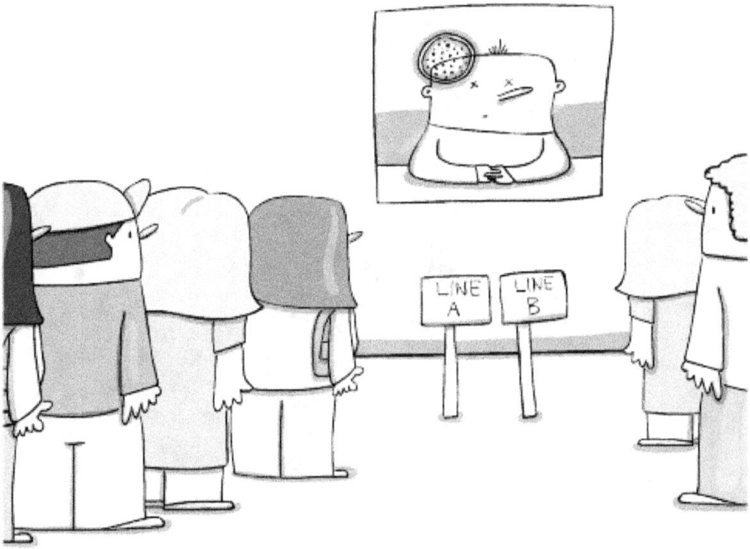
LINE A
LINE B

II.

Ceiling fan.

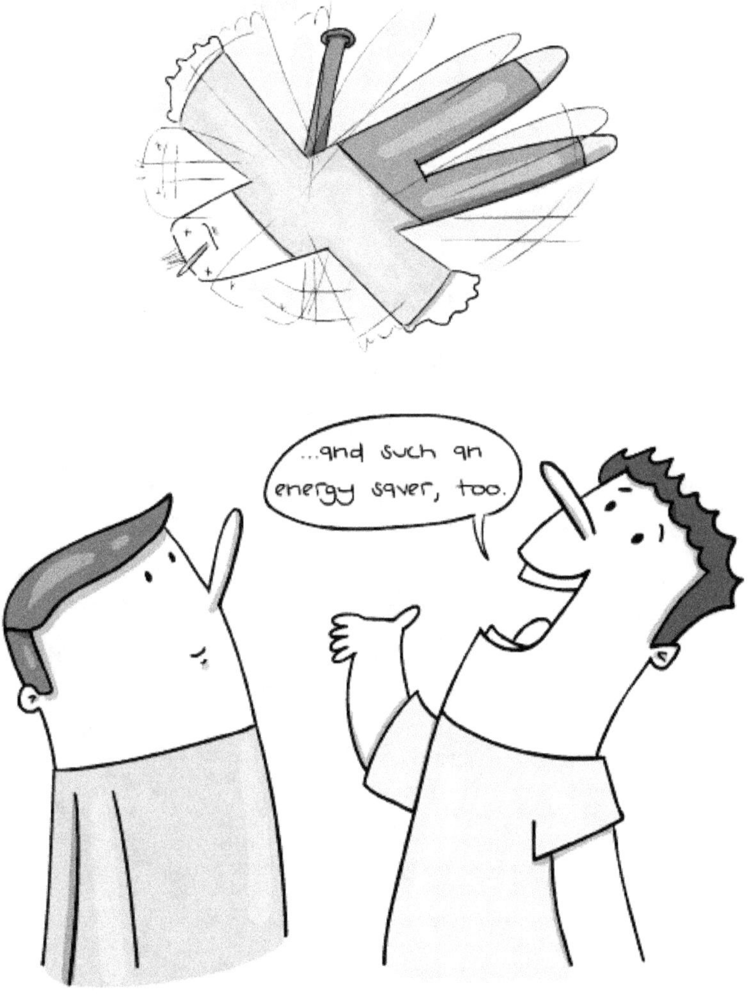
...and such an energy saver, too.

12.

Amusement park buddy so no one sits alone.

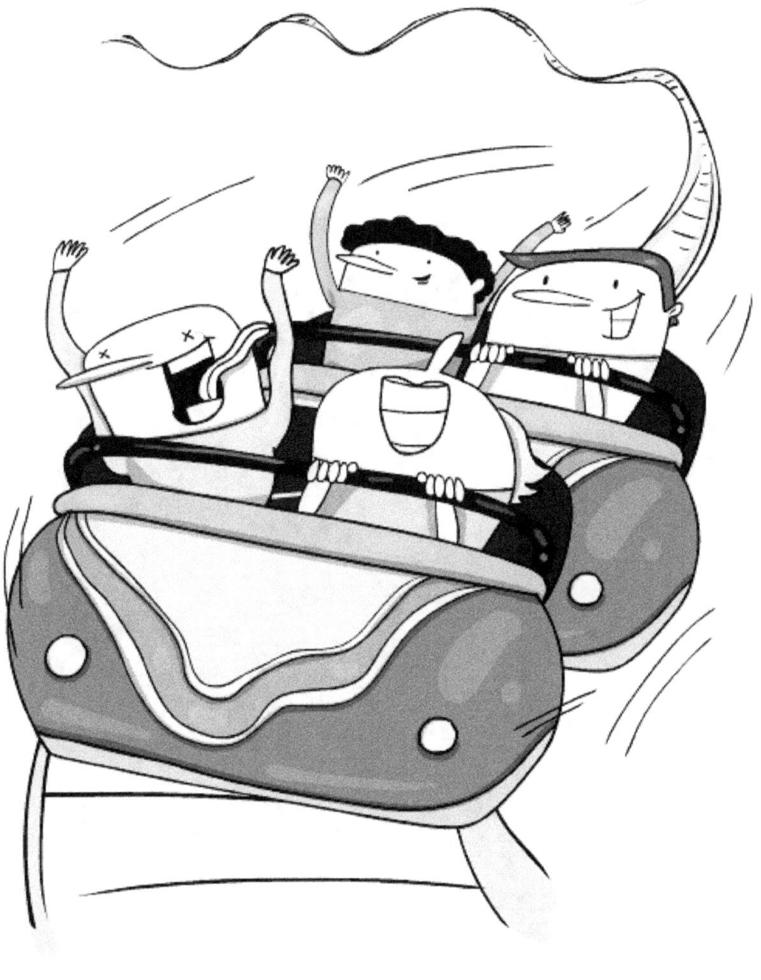

13.

As a prop to drive in the HOV (high occupancy vehicle) lane.

14.

A a sandbag for when the river floods again.

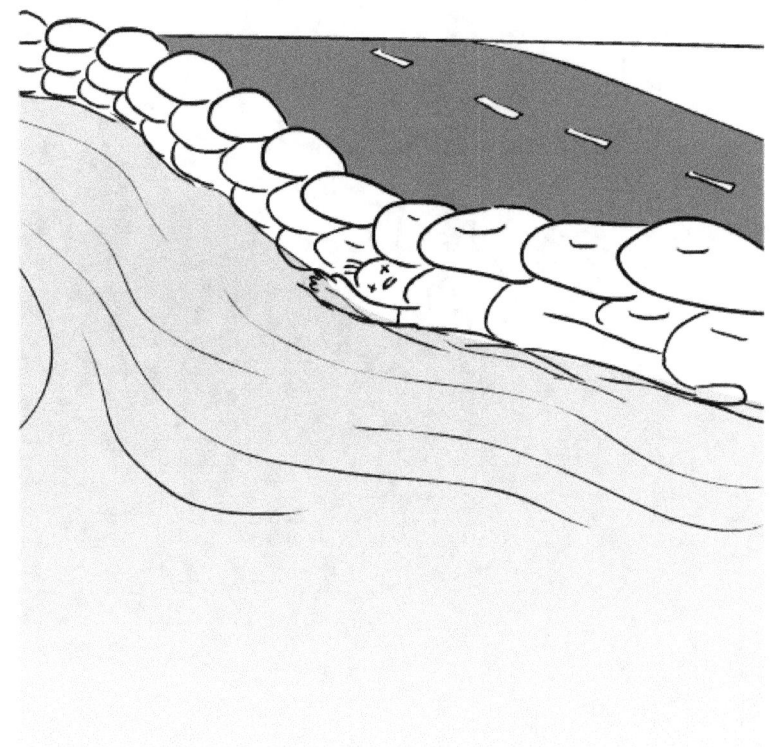

15.

To intimidate men who won't support the ERA or equal pay for women.

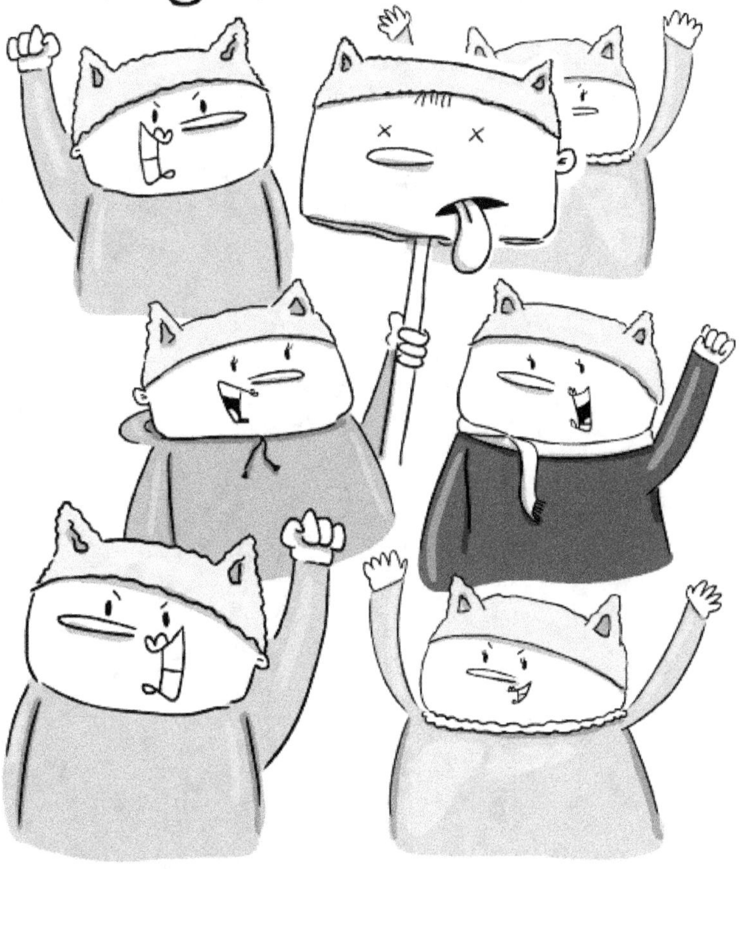

16.

An Olympic weightlifting partner.

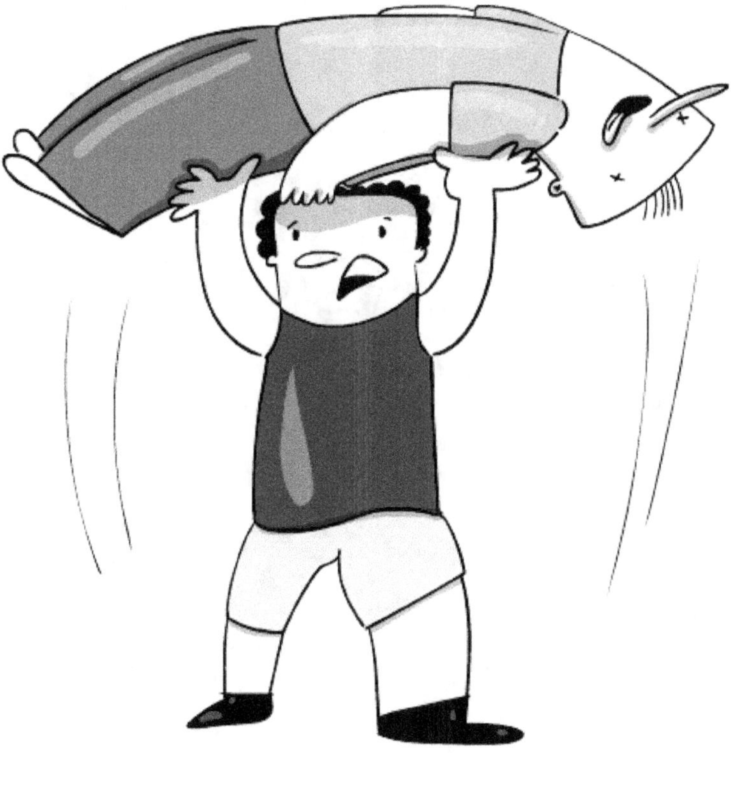

17.

Catapult filler.

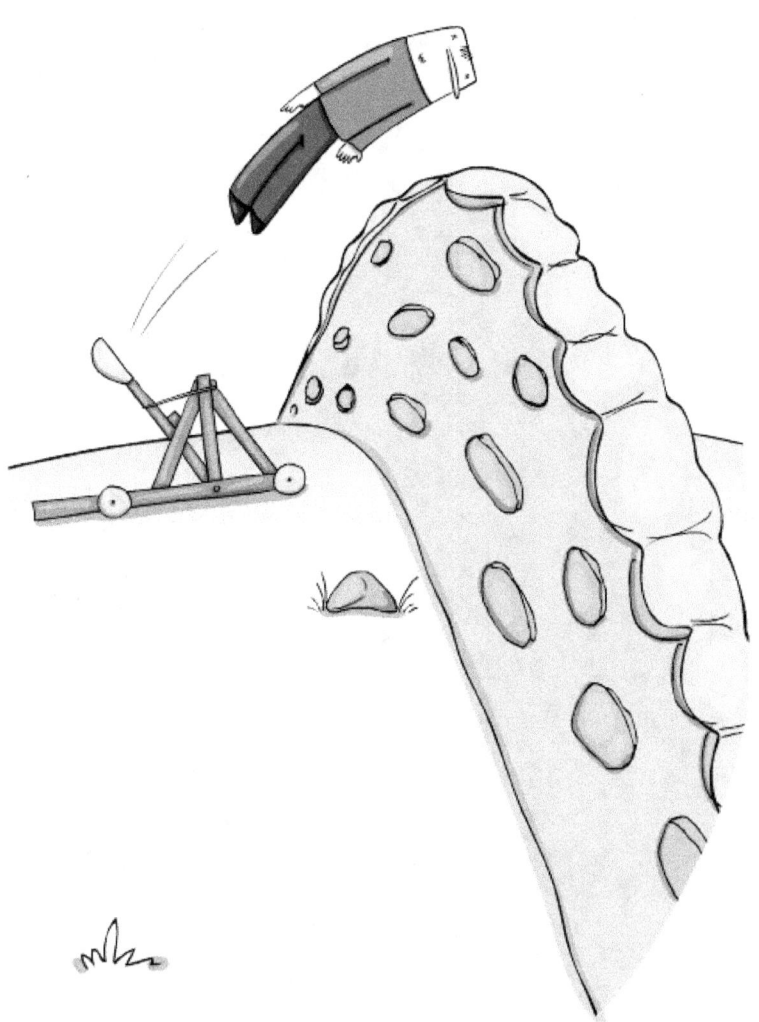

18.

To leave in your place when you escape prison.

19.

A Boat anchor.

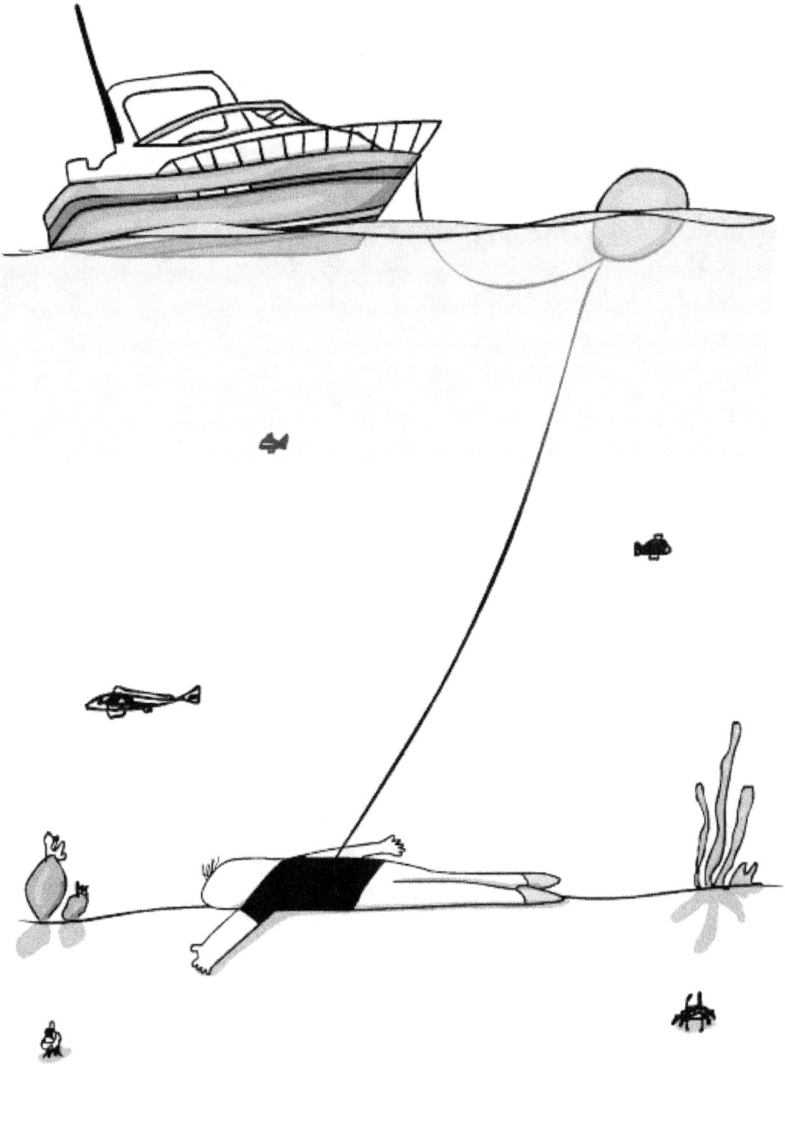

20.

To discourage break-ins while on vacation.

21.

Relay race partner.

22.

Star of the new

TV show

about zombies.

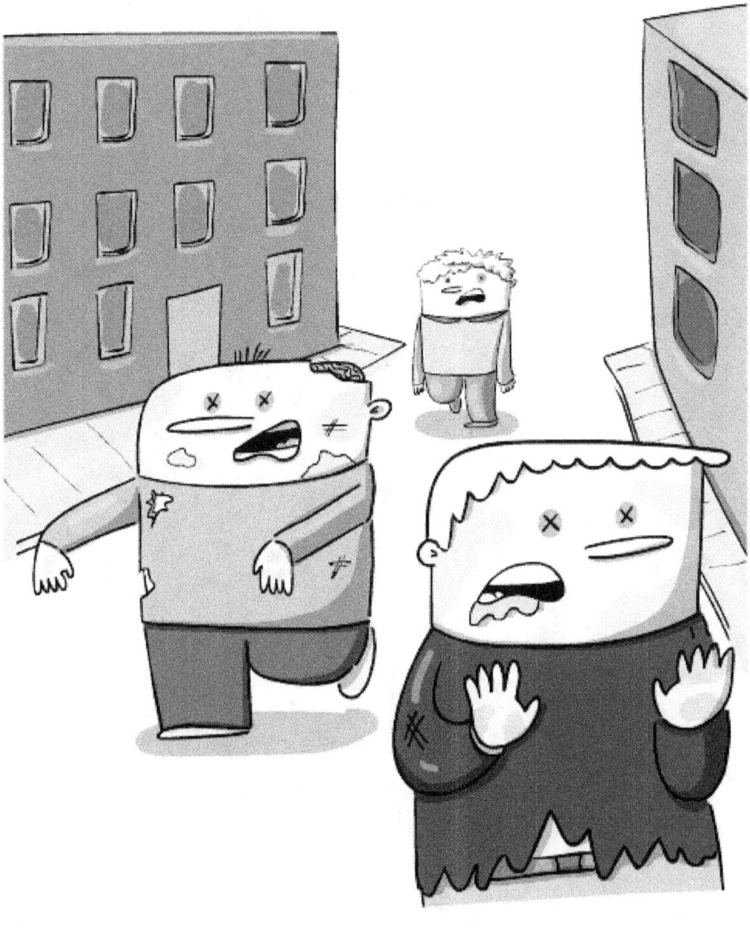

23.

A Sled.

24.

A Pool float.

25.

Cat scratching post.

26.

A Christmas tree.

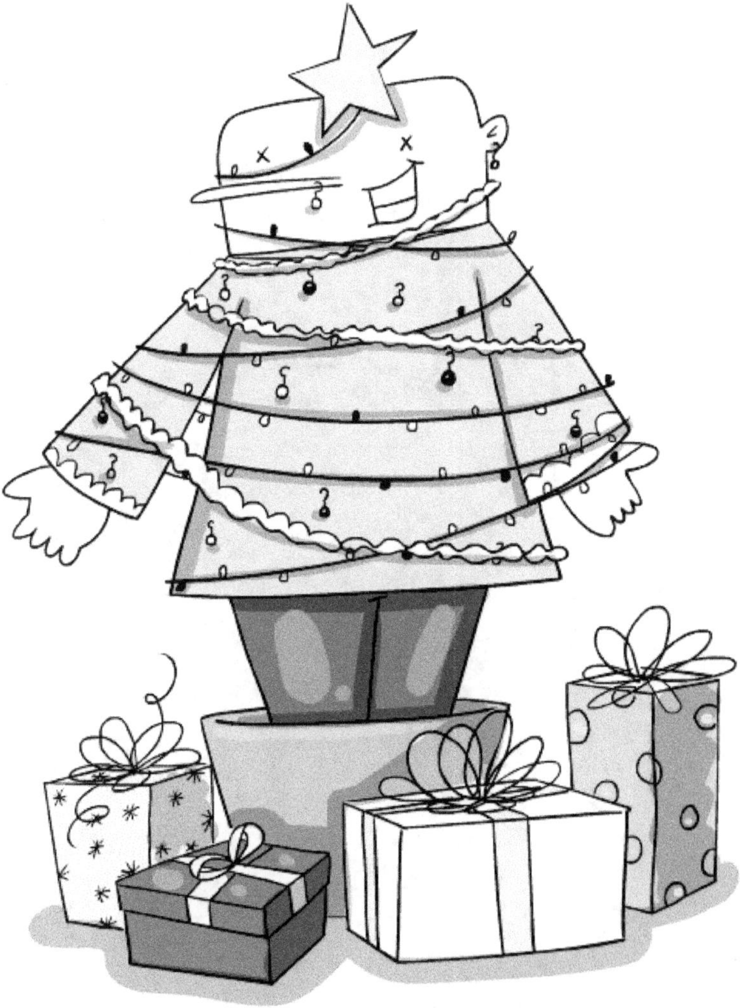

27.

A Substitute teacher.

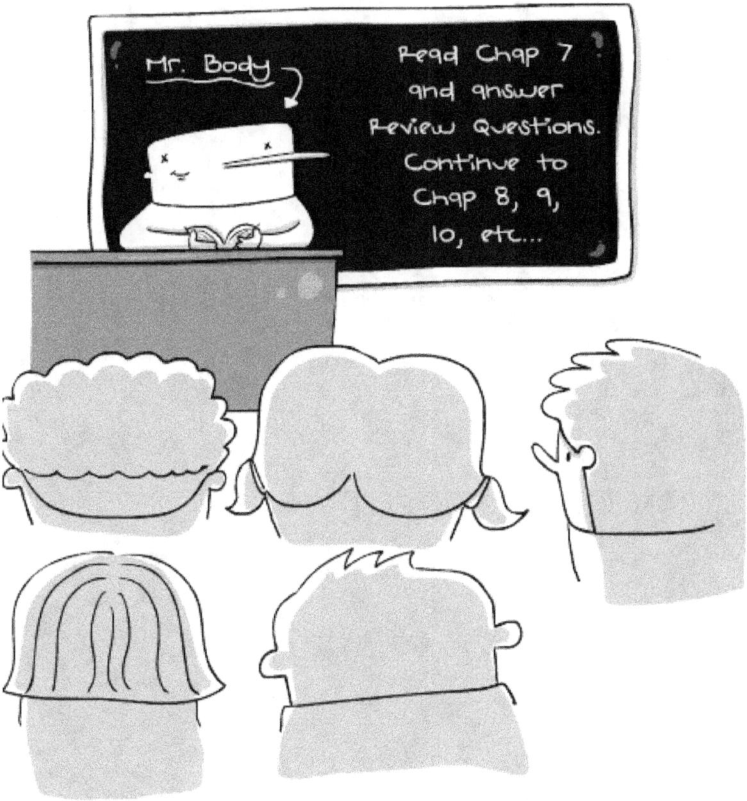
Mr. Body
Read Chap 7 and answer Review Questions. Continue to Chap 8, 9, 10, etc...

28.

car jack.

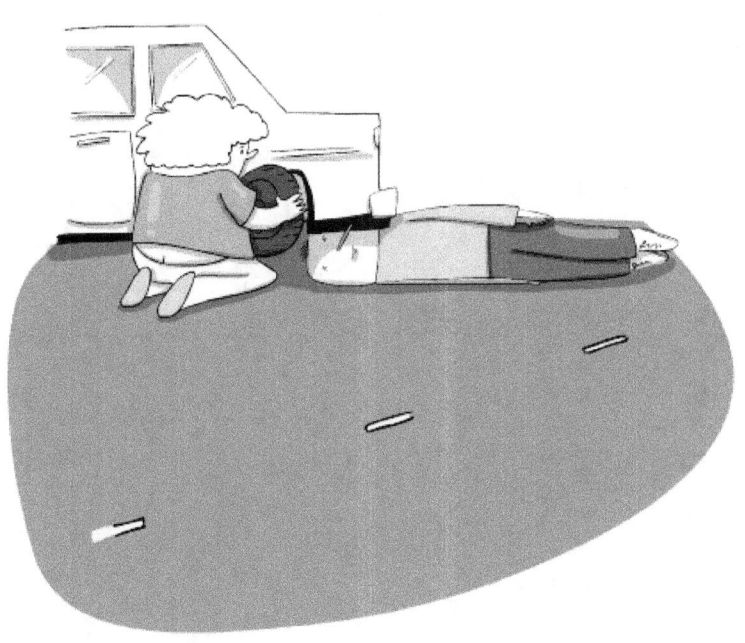

29.

walmart greeter.

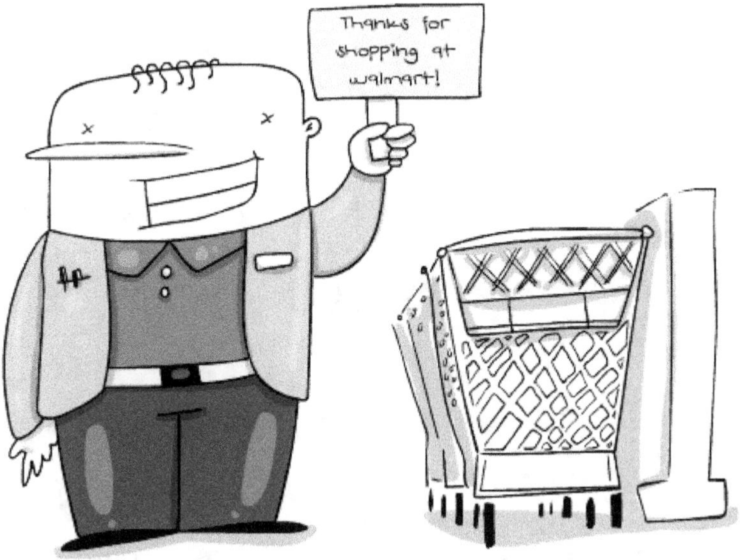
Thanks for shopping at walmart!

30.

Punching bag.

31.

Stunt double.

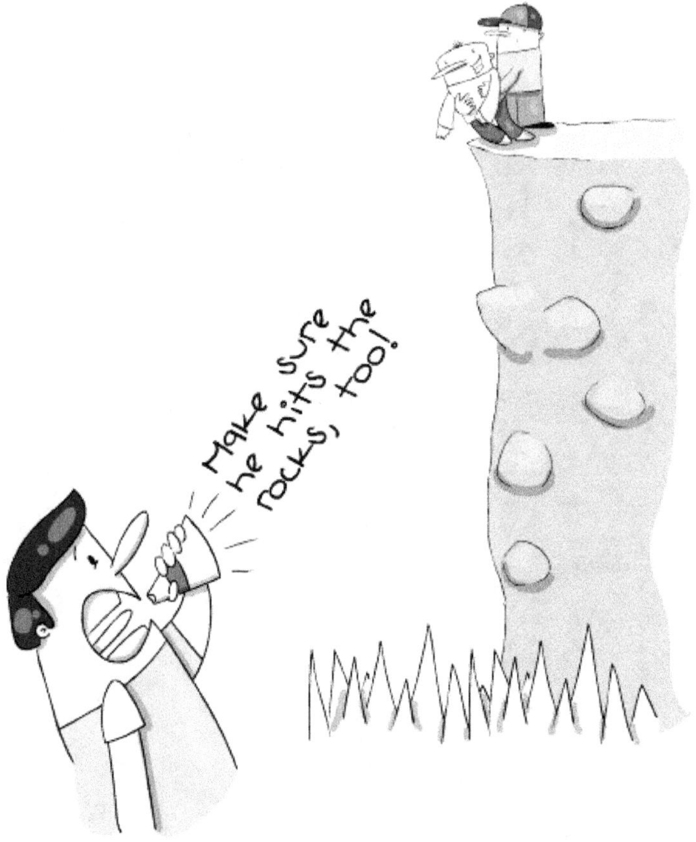
Make sure he hits the rocks, too!

32.

Store mannequin.

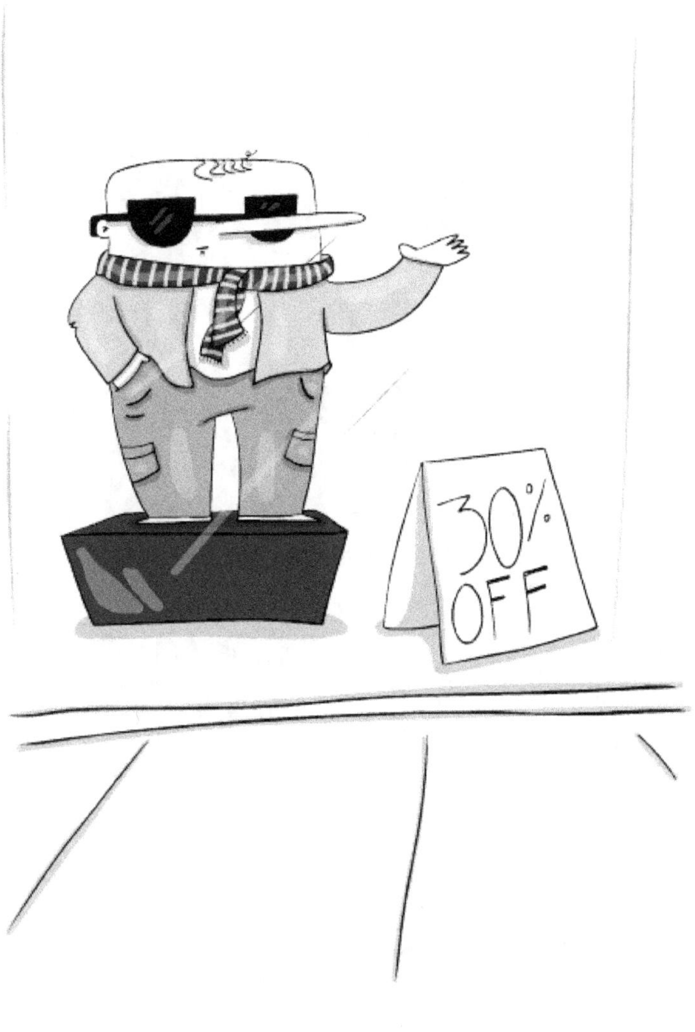
30%
OFF

33.

Speed bump.

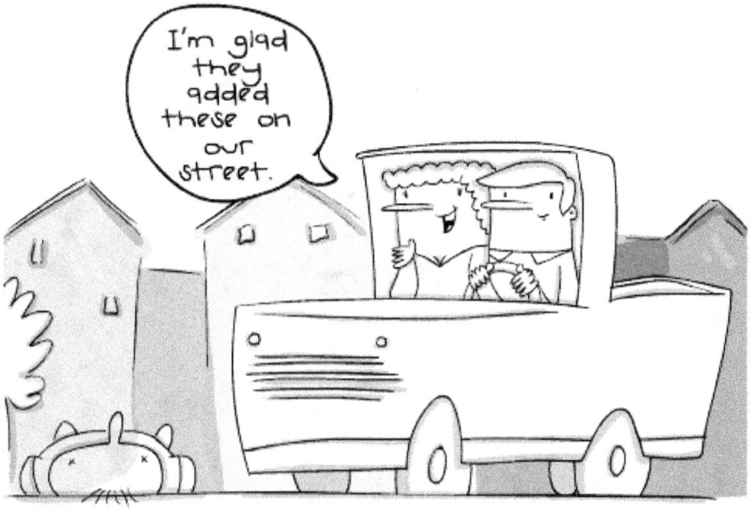
I'm glad they added these on our street.

34.

Paper weight.

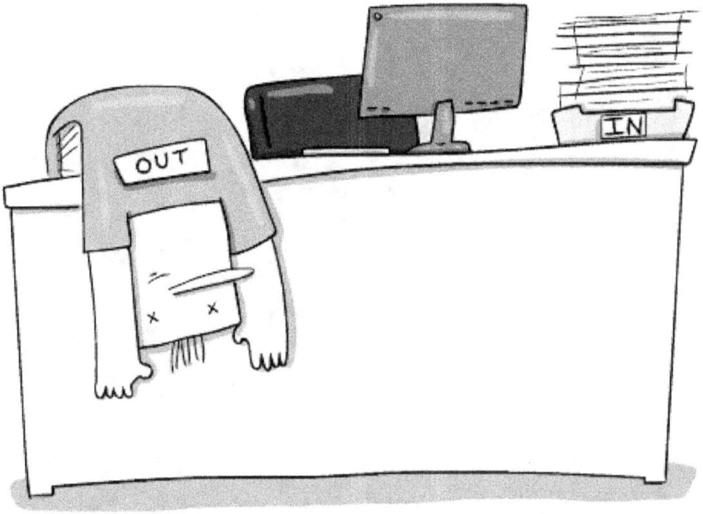
OUT
IN

35.

To charge your devices.

36.

To balance out the tenor section of the church choir.

#37.

Booster seat.

38.

A crossfit gym obstacle.

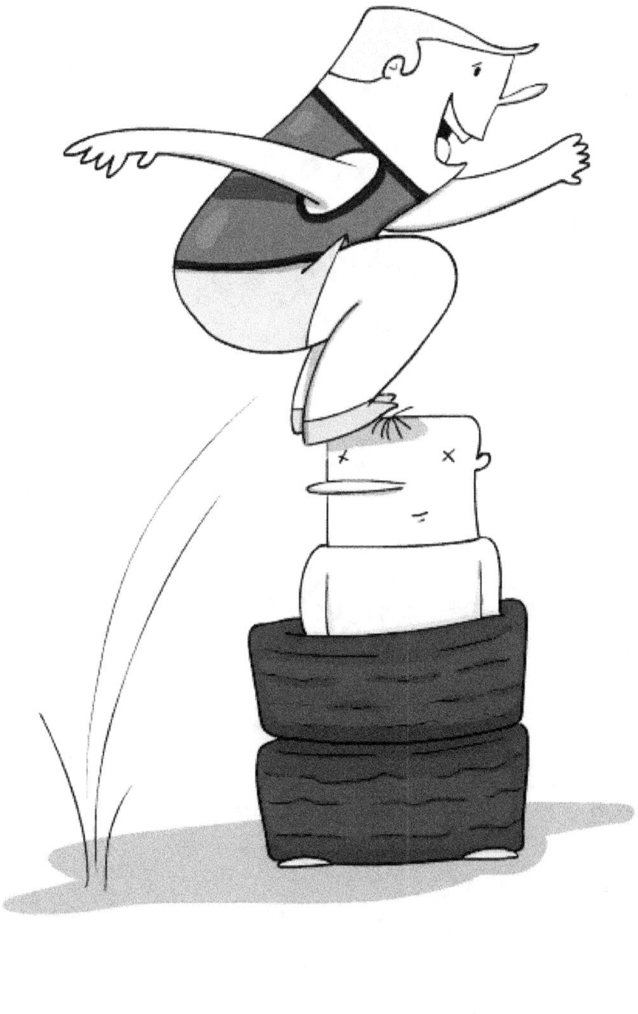

39.

A place to put your car keys where you'll never forget.

40.

Hiking buddy.

41.

To hold your seat while you get concessions.

42.

A substitute for a costly scuba weight system.

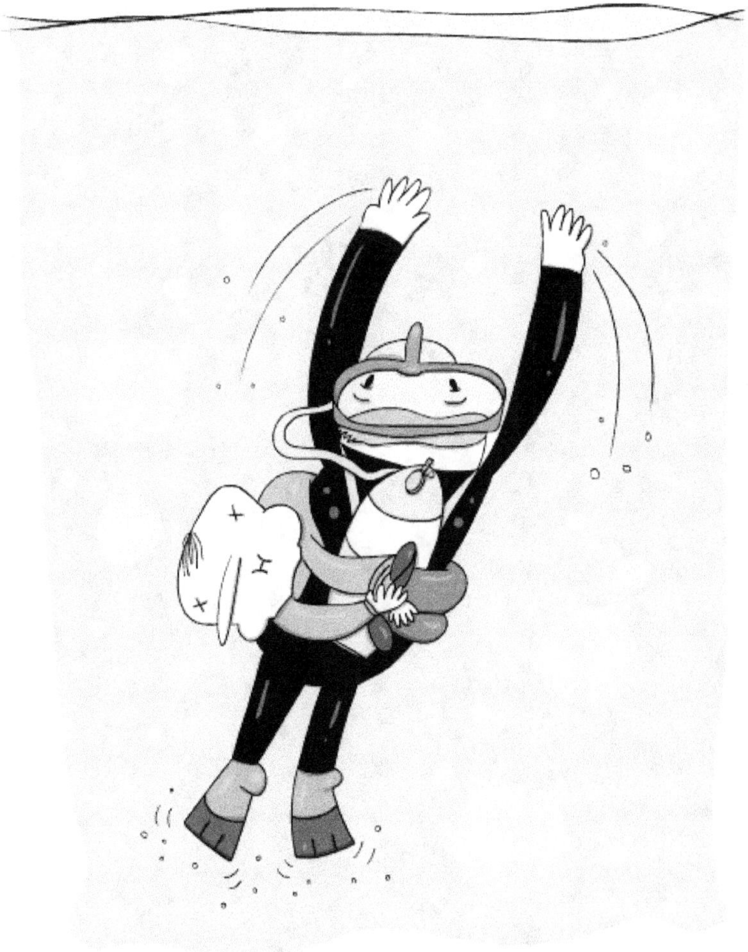

43.

Extra furniture in the guest bedroom you never finished decorating.

44.

Coffee table.

45.

Art.

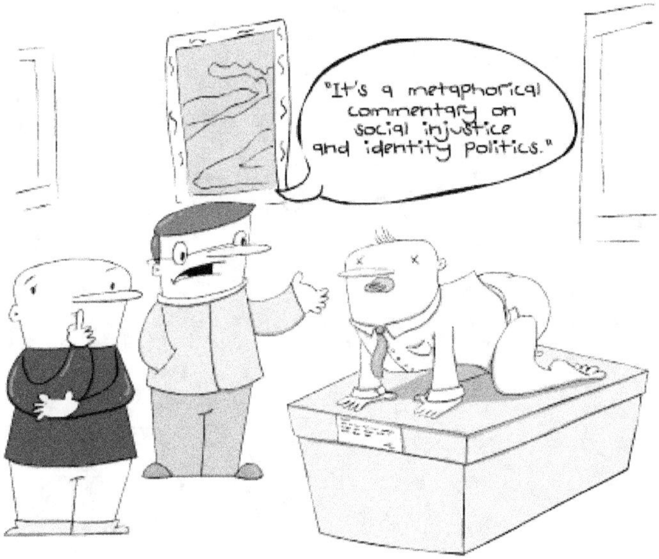
"It's a metaphorical commentary on social injustice and identity politics."

46.

Last minute babysitter.

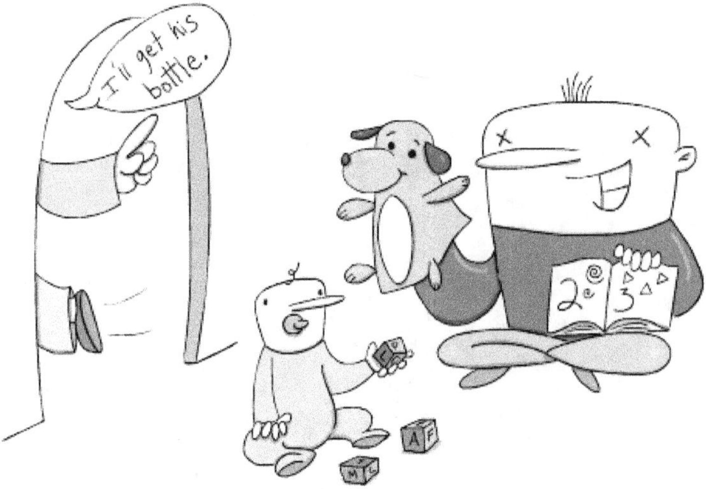
I'll get his bottle.

47.

for hanging clothes.

48.

Someone who will finally listen to you without bringing the conversation back to himself.

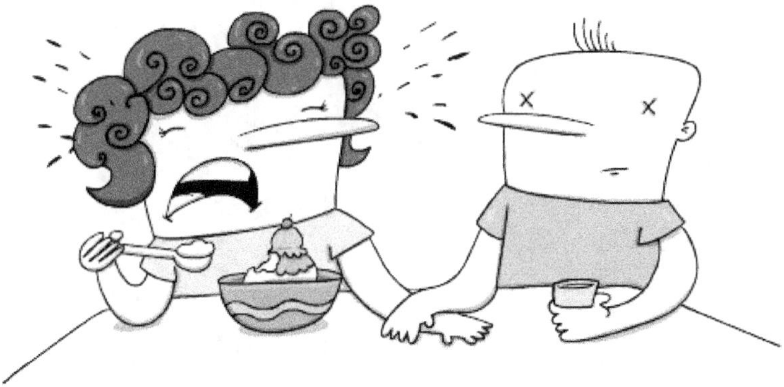

49.

An emotional support animal.

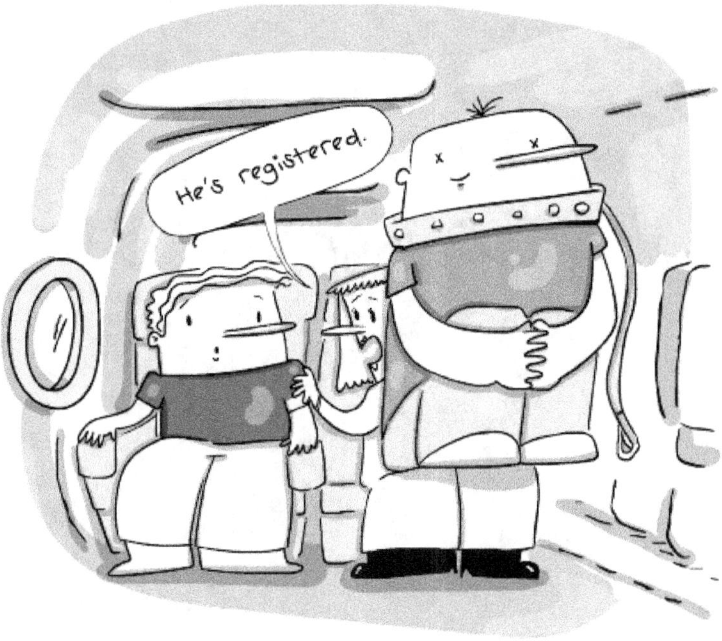
He's registered.

50.

A practice partner for dangerous acrobatic maneuvers.

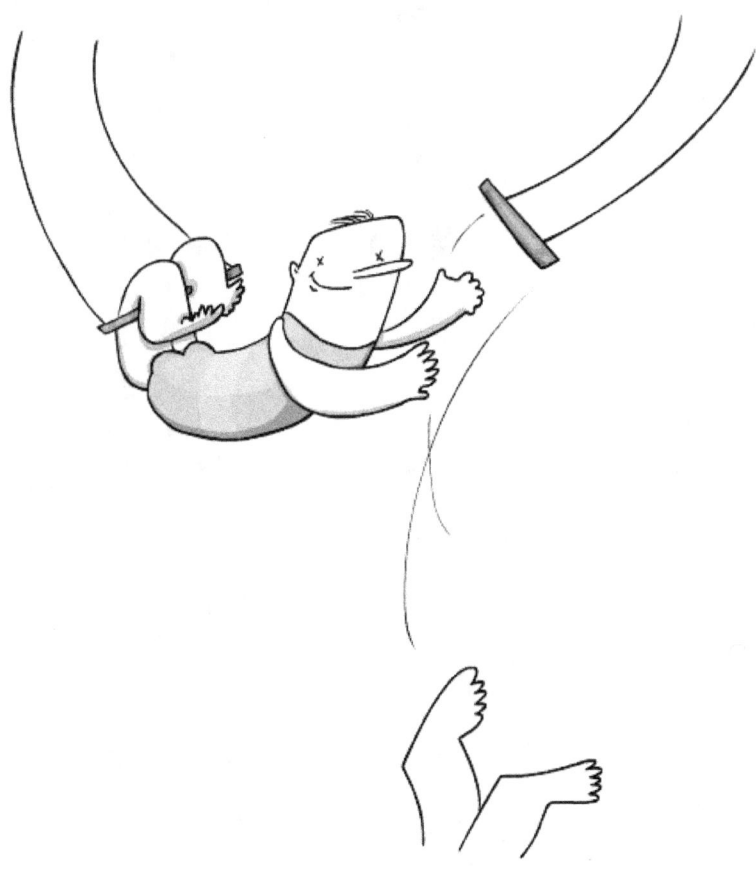

51.

To cover the odor of what you just did in the bathroom.

52.

Basketball.

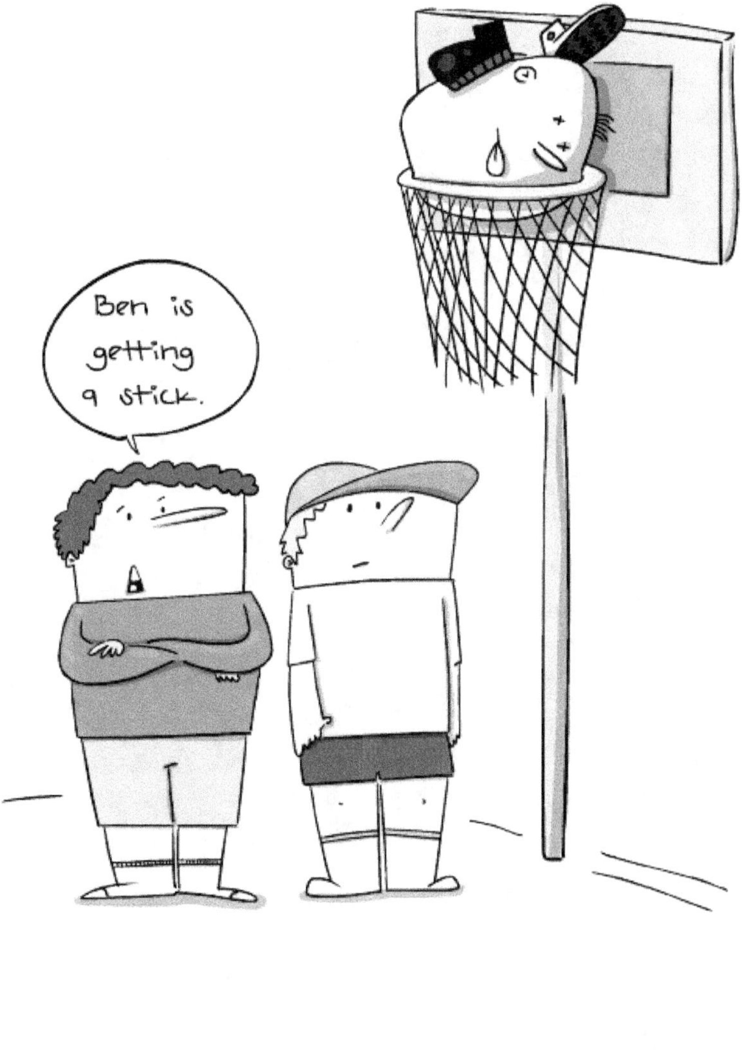
Ben is getting a stick.

53.

A fun prank at the office to break up the monotony of the daily grind.

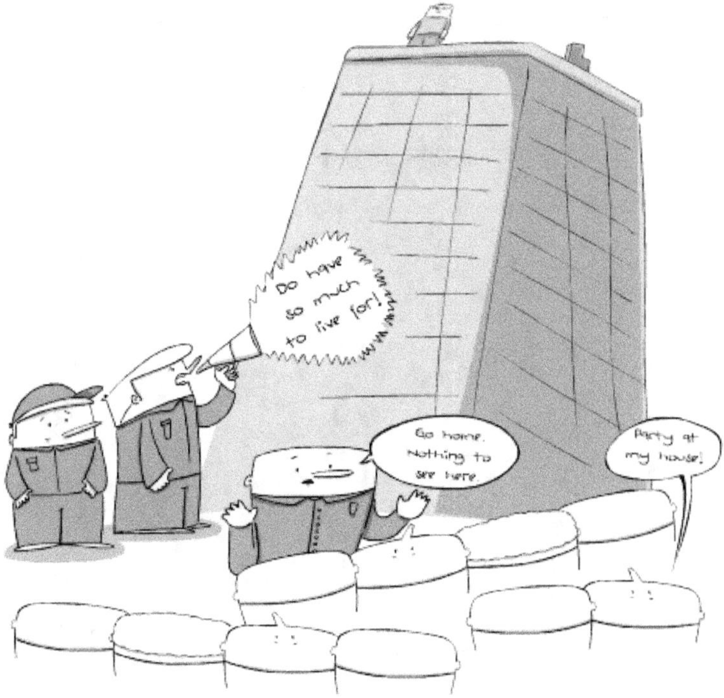
Do have so much to live for!
Go home. Nothing to see here.
Party at my house!

54.

To sit next to your crazy, drunk uncle at Thanksgiving.

55.

Casket model

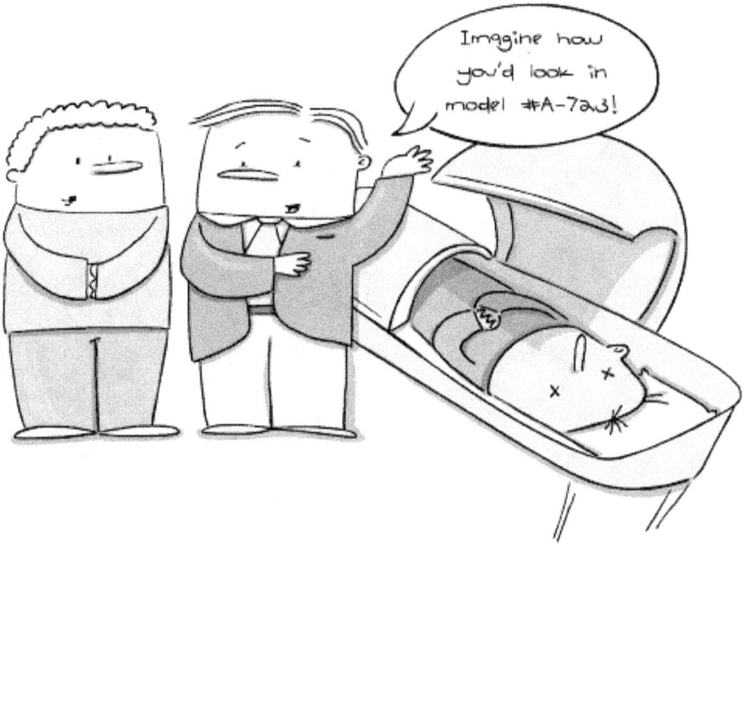
Imagine how you'd look in model #A-723!

56.

Extra in a huge Hollywood blockbuster

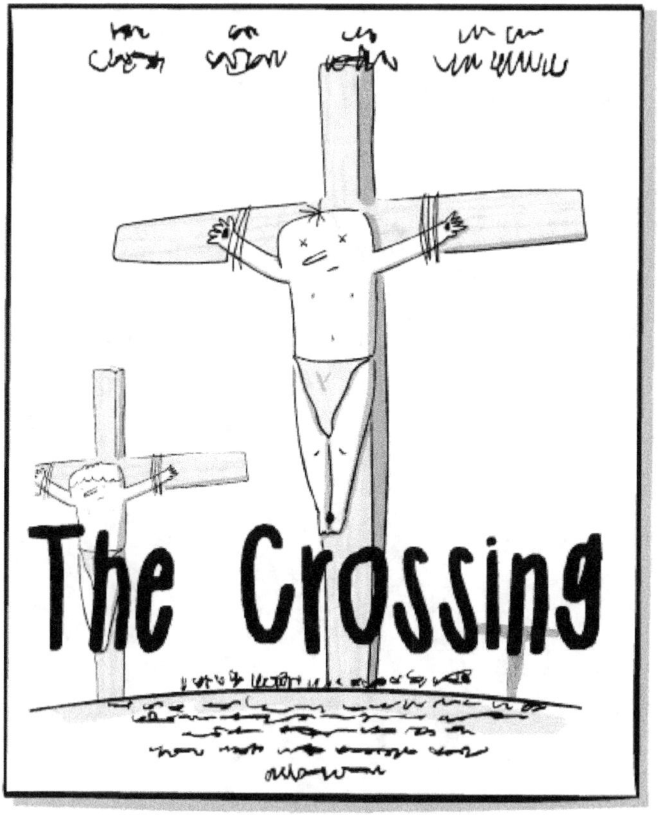
The Crossing

57.

A reason to leave the party early.

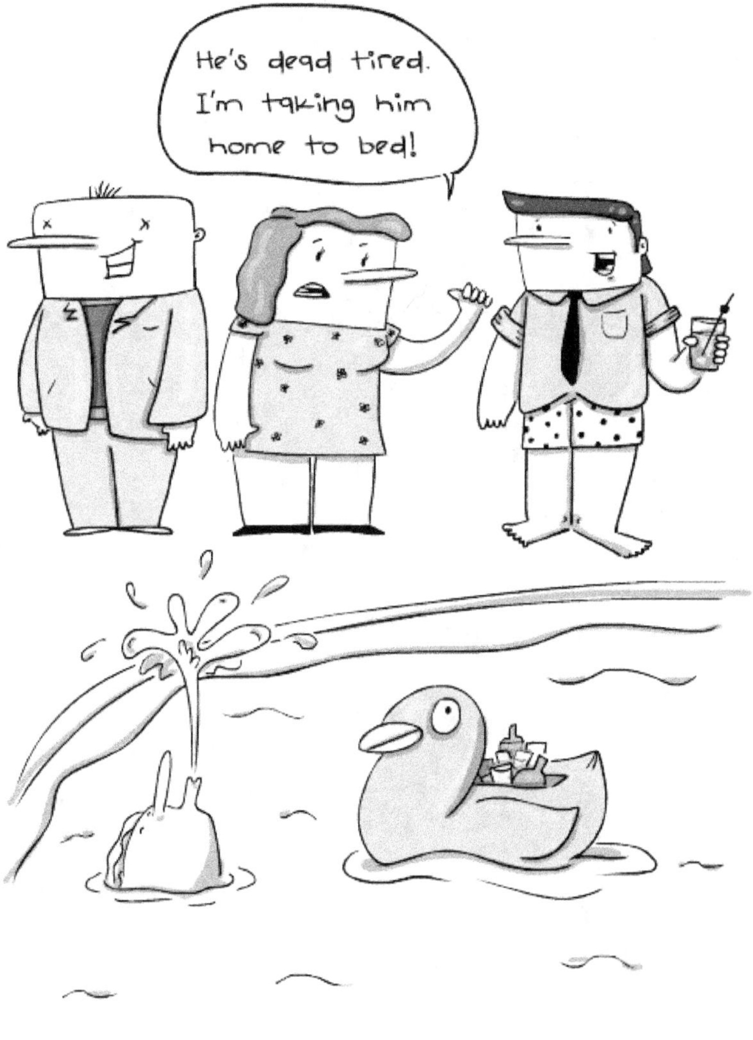
He's dead tired. I'm taking him home to bed!

58.

Car salesman.

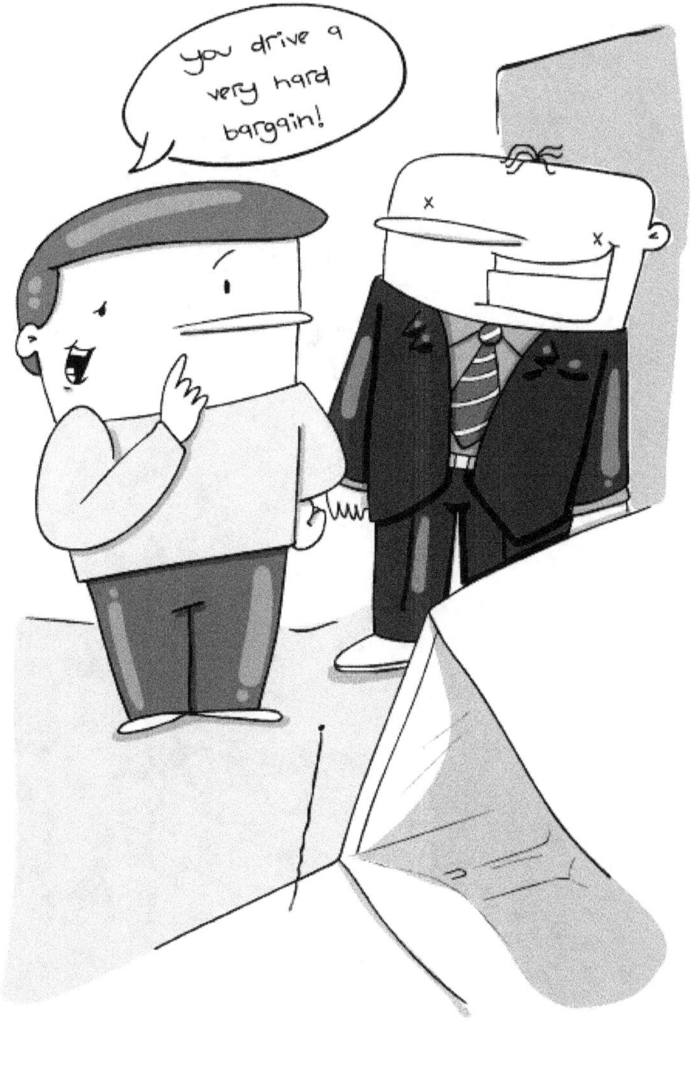
you drive a very hard bargain!

59.

To hold your place on the phone with customer service.

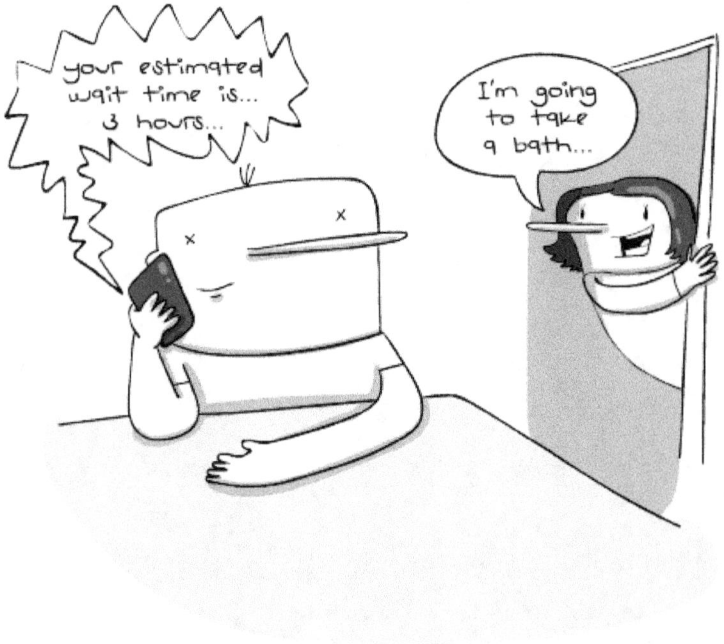
your estimated wait time is... 3 hours...
I'm going to take a bath...

# 60.

An alibi for the night of the incident.

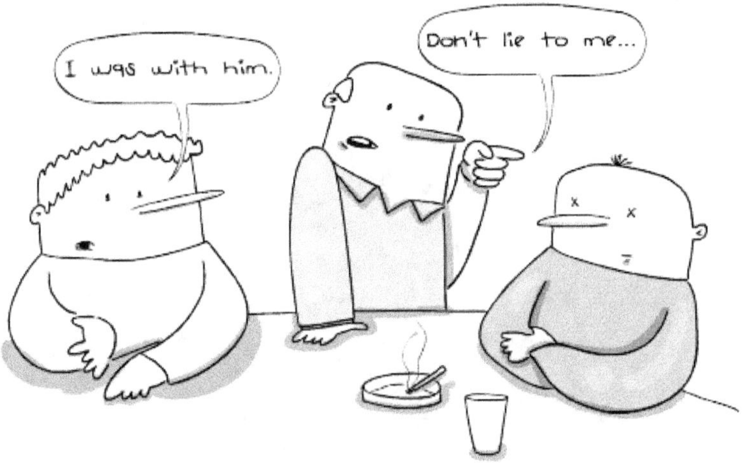
I was with him.
Don't lie to me...

#61.

Because you've given up on dating and don't want to die alone.

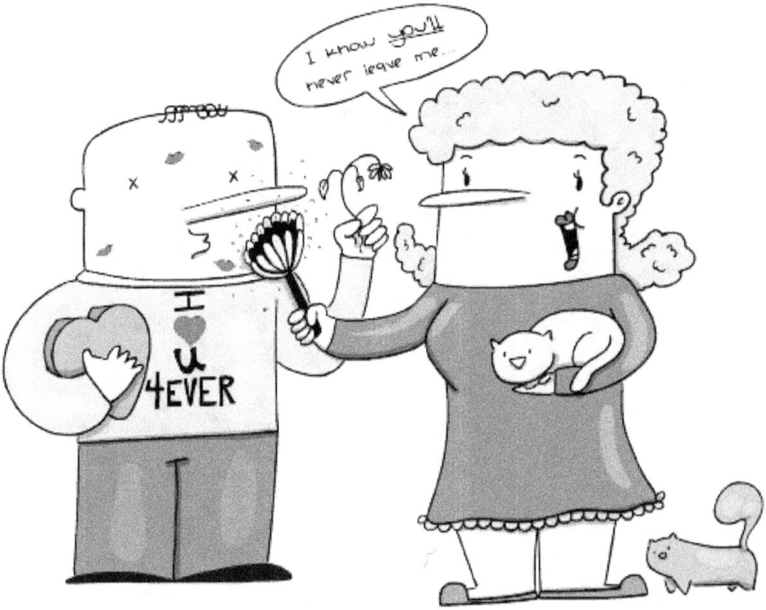
I know you'll never leave me...
I ♥ U 4EVER

62.

To help you discipline your kids.

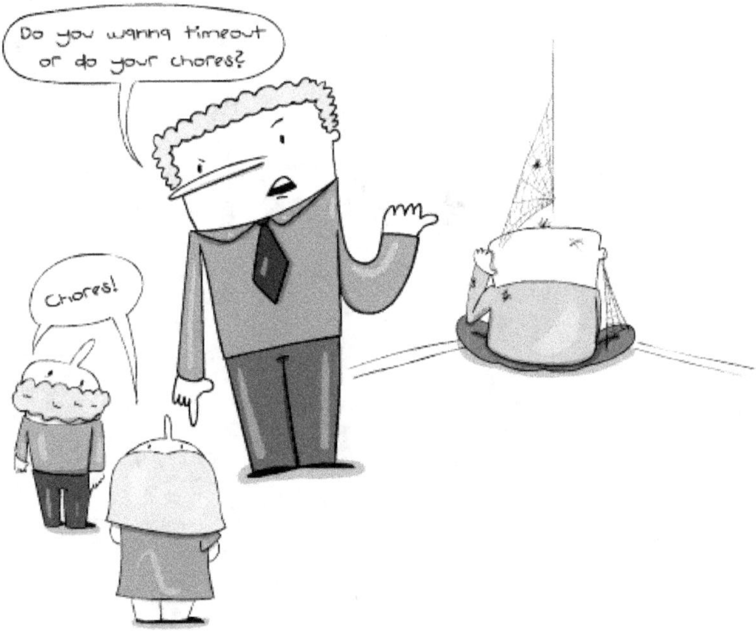
Do you wanna timeout or do your chores?
Chores!

#63.

Part of your possé.

64.

Playmate for only child.

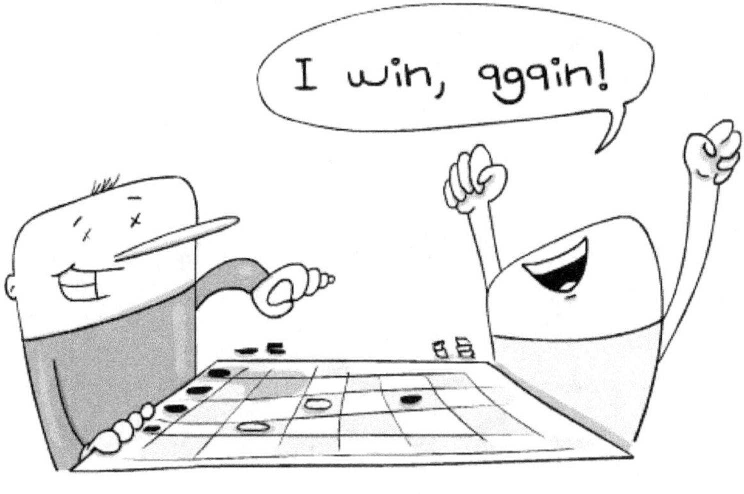
I win, again!

65.

Date for a formal work event.

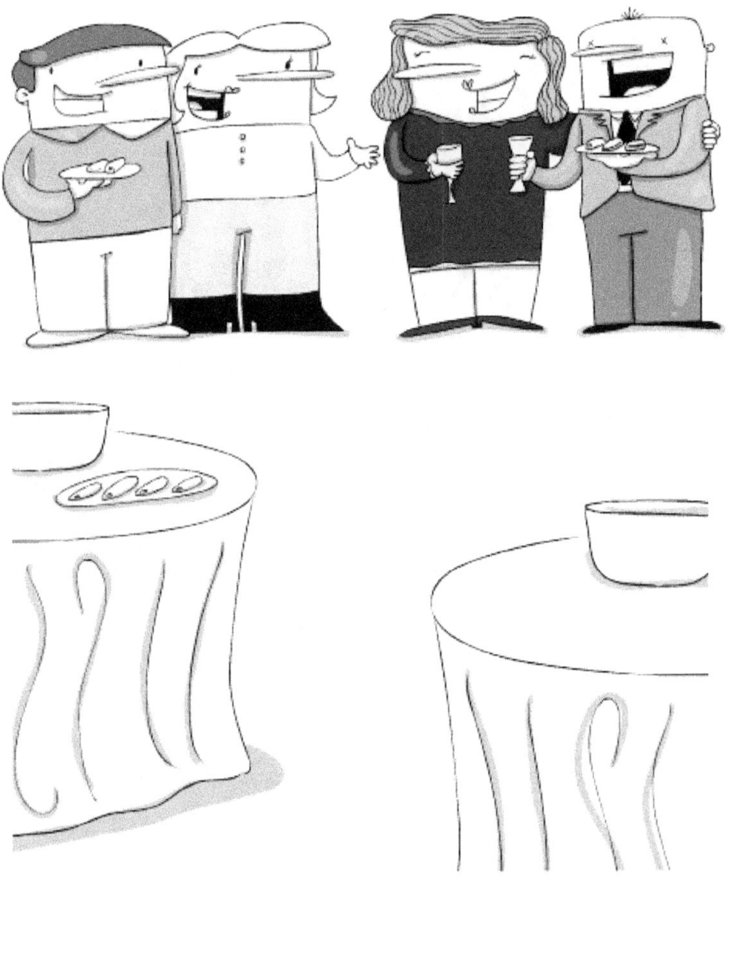

66.

Cult member.

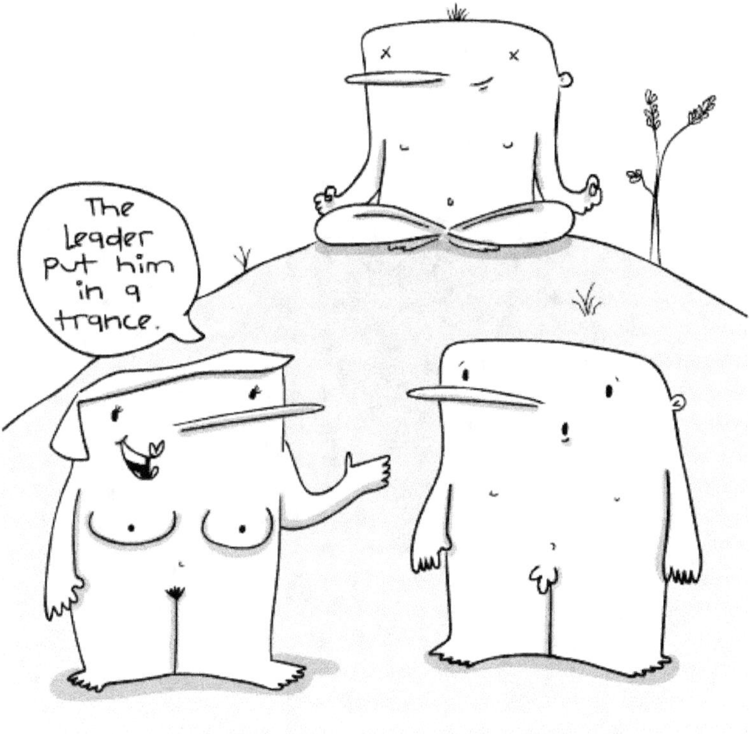
The leader put him in a trance.

67.

Cult leader.

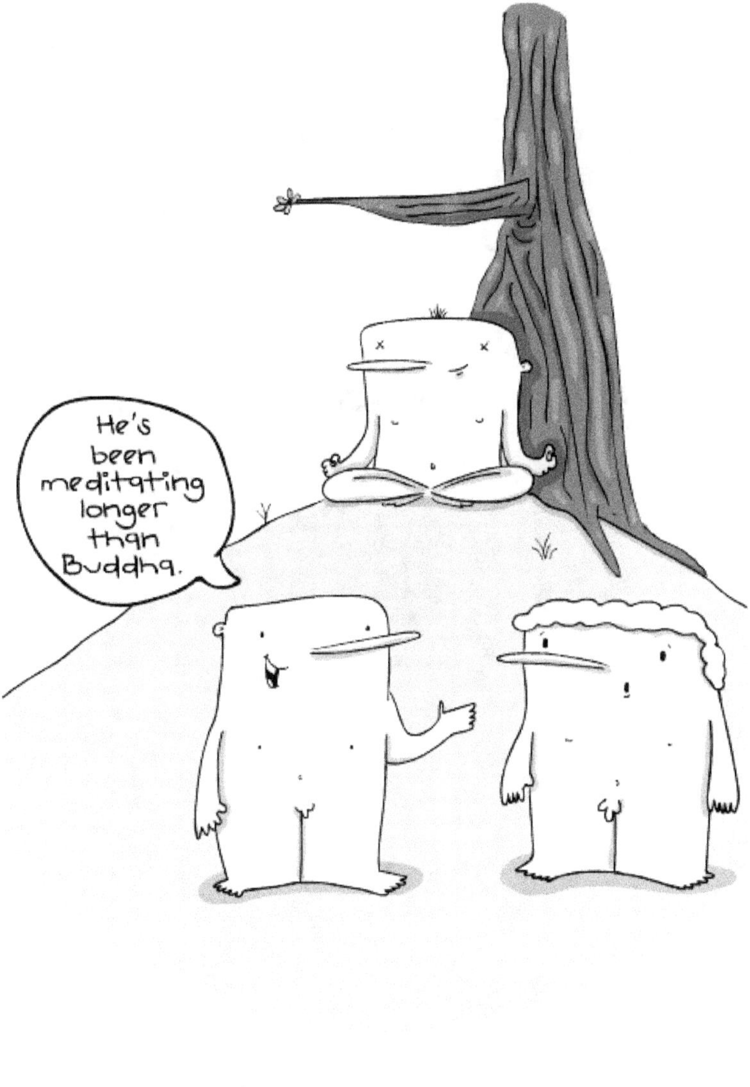
He's been meditating longer than Buddha.

68.

So you don't
have to watch
that movie all alone.

69.

Reality TV star.

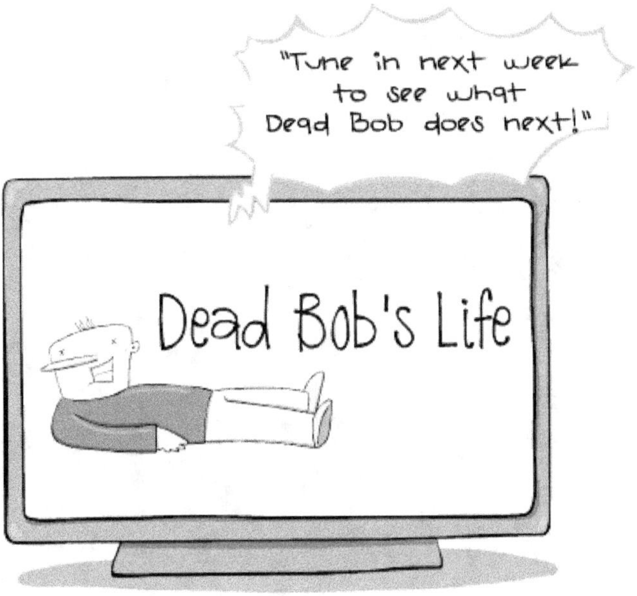
"Tune in next week to see what Dead Bob does next!"
Dead Bob's Life

70.

Pretend friend at work so you don't get stuck in a conversation with Marge.

71.

To boost your Twitter followers.

DeadBody
@DeadBody

Tweets 0 Following YOU Followers 0

72.

Dart board.

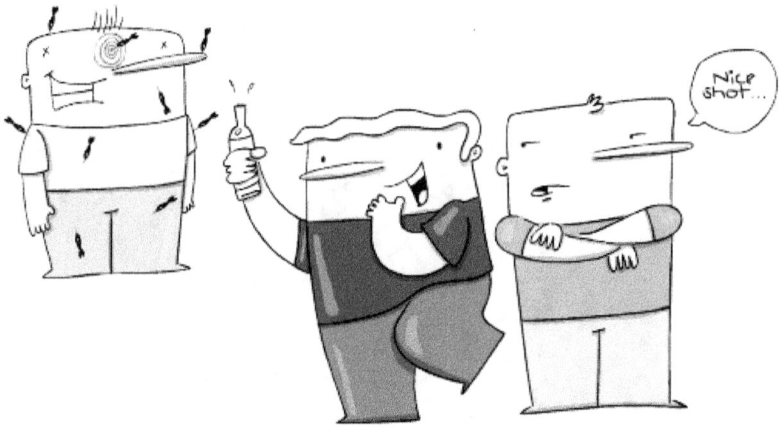
Nice shot...

#73.

Compost starter.

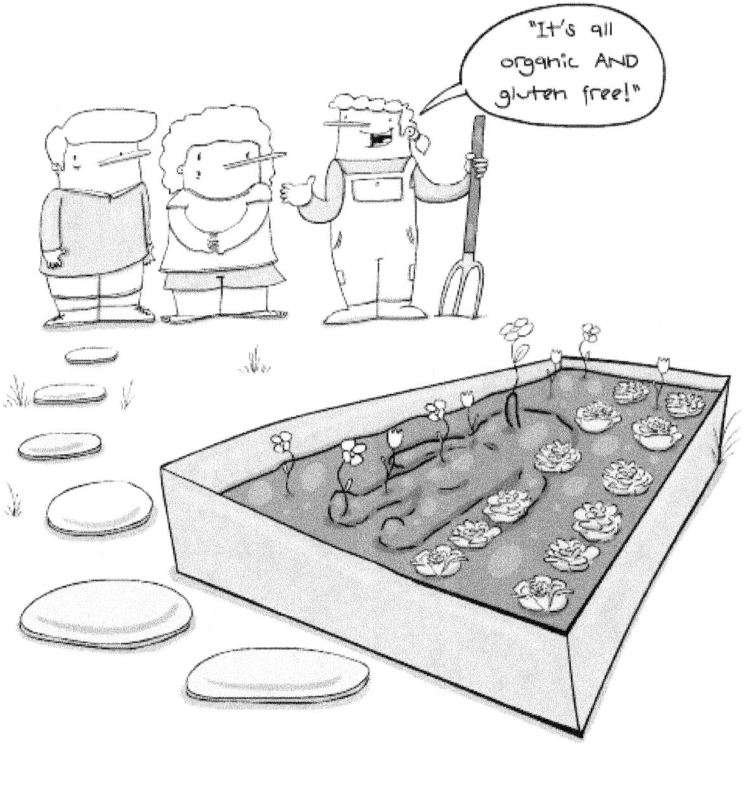
"It's all organic AND gluten free!"

74.

Seesaw partner.

75.

To make your boyfriend jealous.

76.

Drinking buddy.

77.

A prospect for your home-based business.

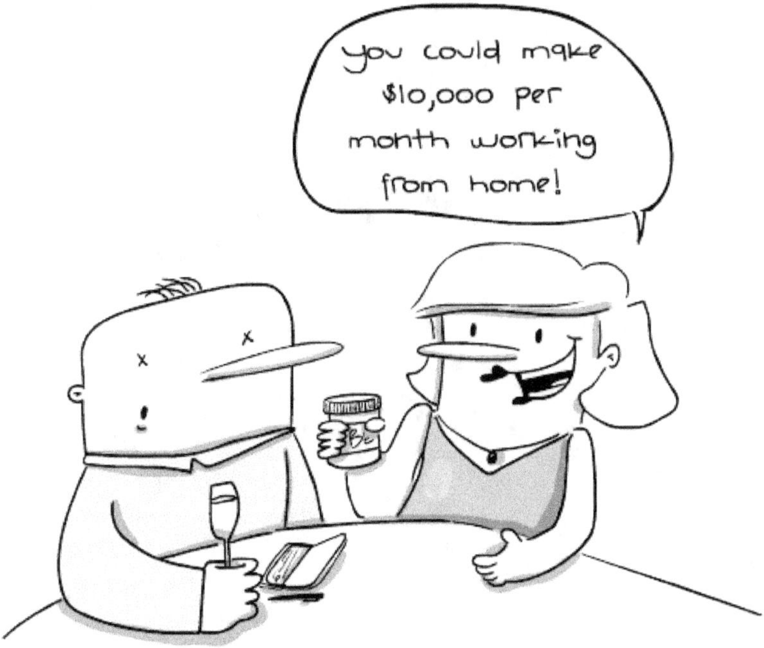
you could make $10,000 per month working from home!

78.

To see if there's any truth to the Frankenstein story.

79.

Wingman
for picking up chicks.

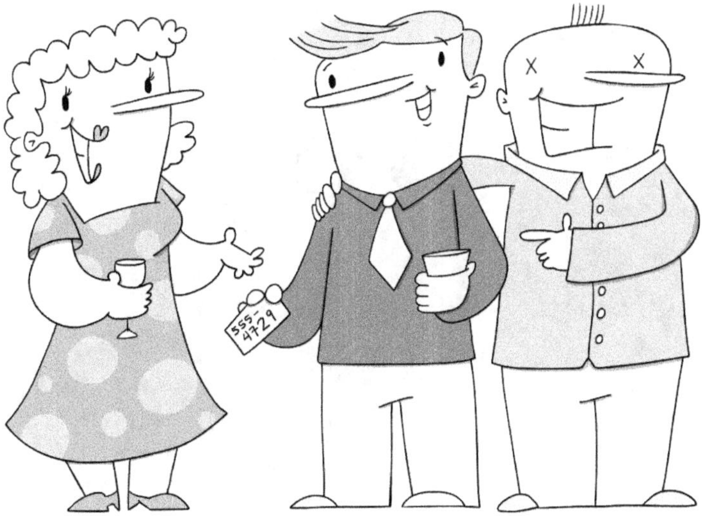
555-
4729

80.

Political pundit on cable news.

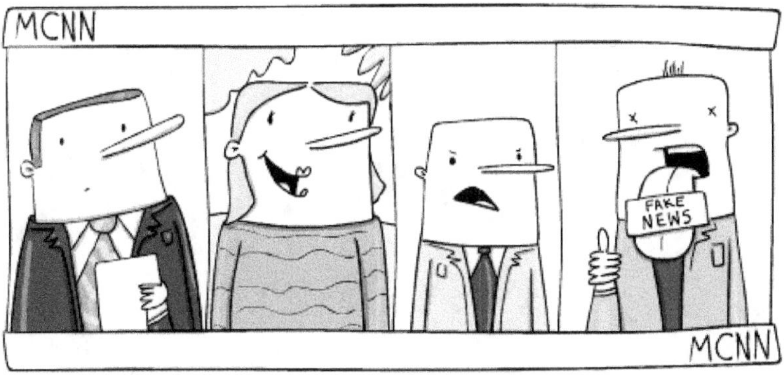
MCNN
FAKE NEWS
MCNN

81.

Cuddle pillow.

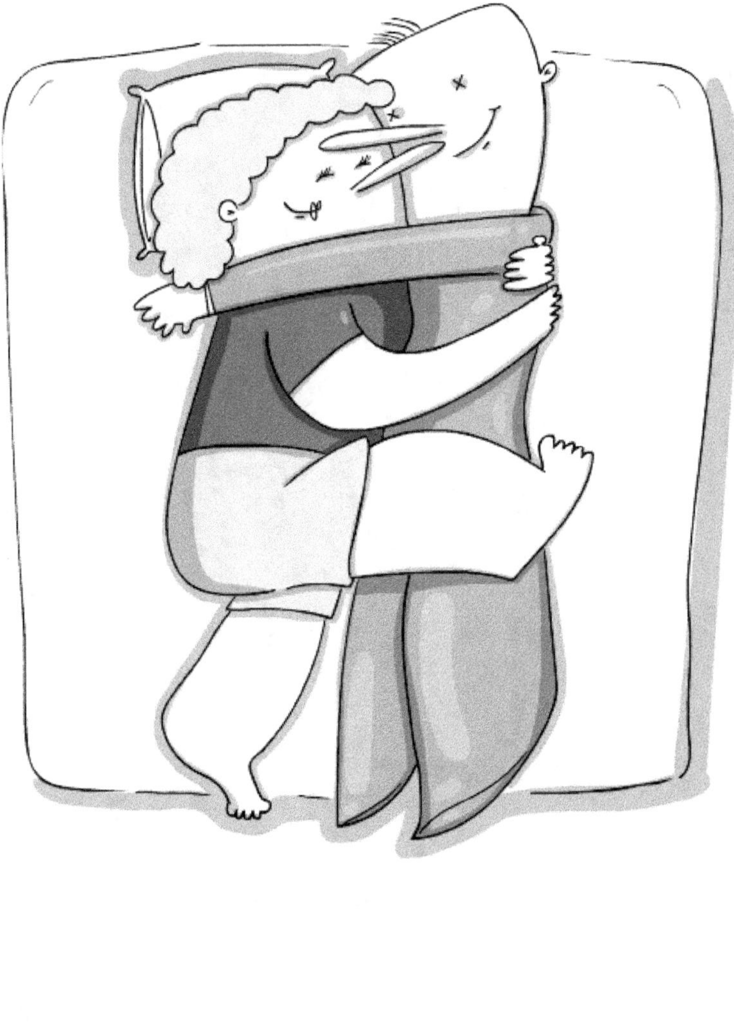

82.

A sit-in at boring work meetings.

83.

One man
who won't violate
your consent.

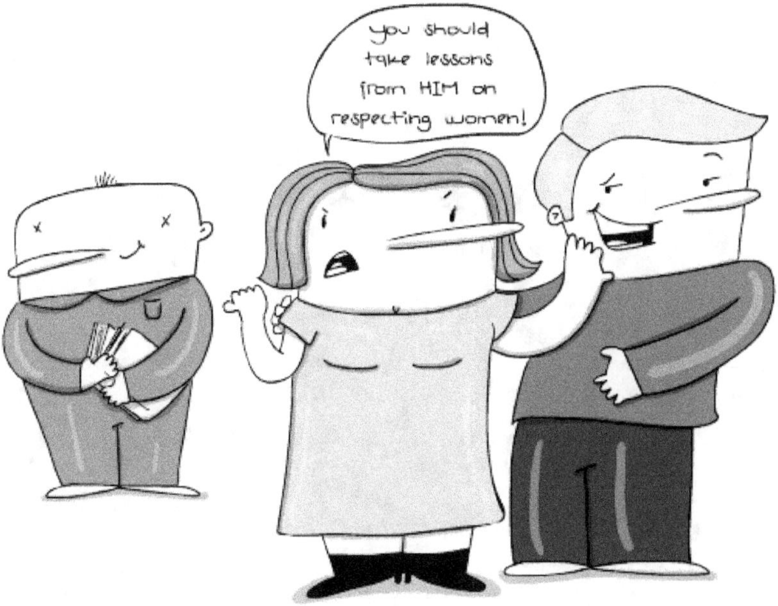
You should take lessons from HIM on respecting women!

84.

White elephant Christmas gift to pass among friends.

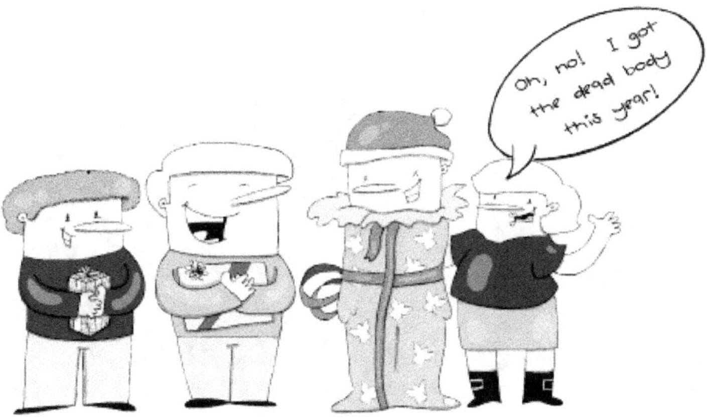
Oh, no! I got the dead body this year!

#85.

Marry it because it'll be the same in about 10 years.

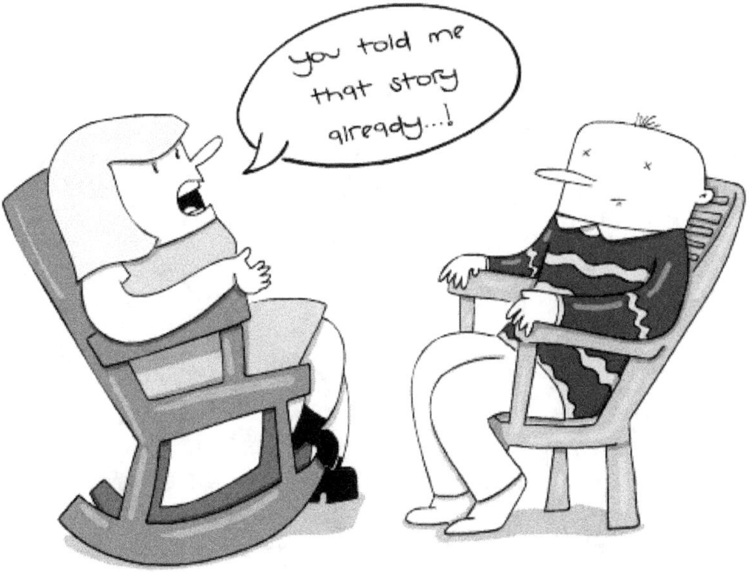
you told me that story already...!

86.

To leave at your ex's front door instead of a flaming bag of dog poo.

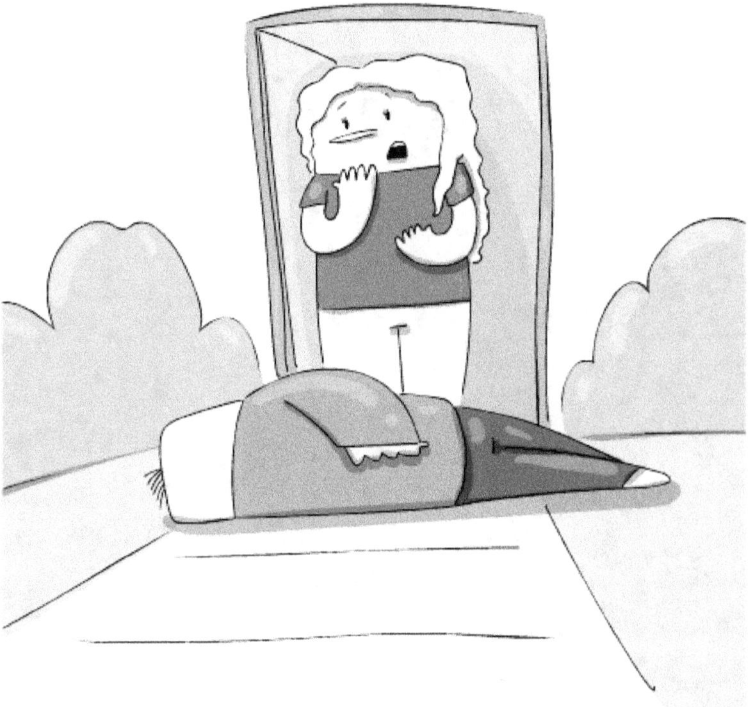

87.

To put in your car trunk so the cops don't find your weed.

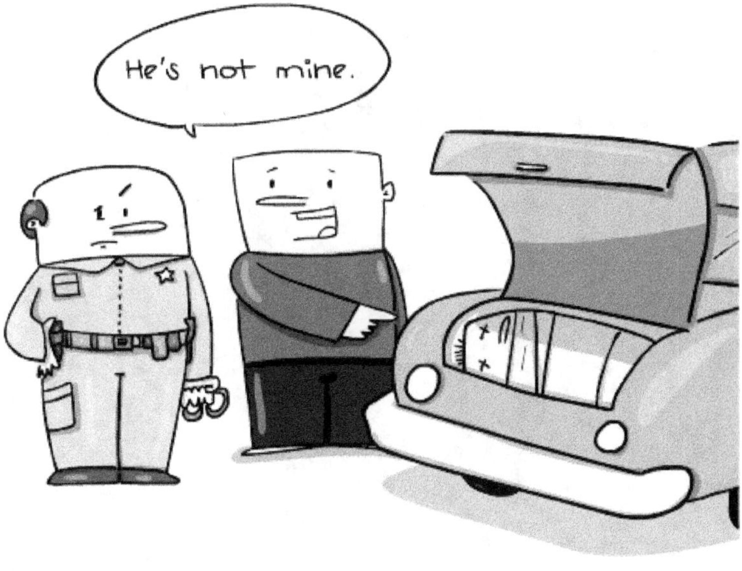
He's not mine.

88.

To finally show the Joneses how a Halloween display should look.

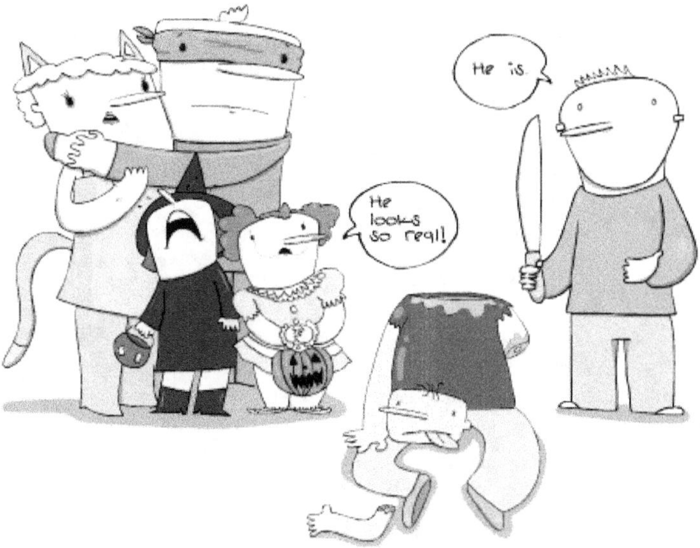
He is.
He looks so real!

89.

Put it in the garage with the other junk you hold onto because it might come in handy someday.

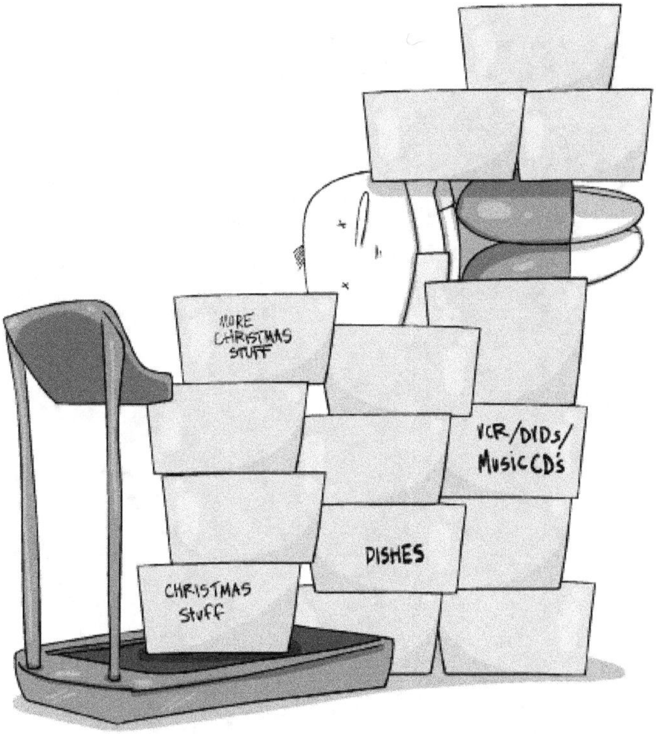
MORE CHRISTMAS STUFF
VCR/DVDs/ MUSIC CD's
DISHES
CHRISTMAS STUFF

90.

Make him leader of the free world.

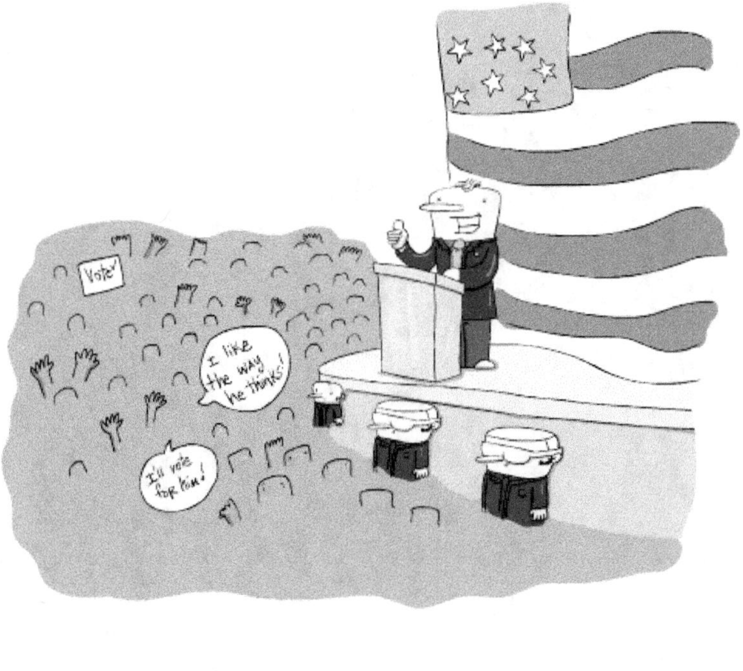
Vote
I like the way he thinks!
I'll vote for him!

91.

Take it to Paris because your husband won't and dammit you're going before you die!

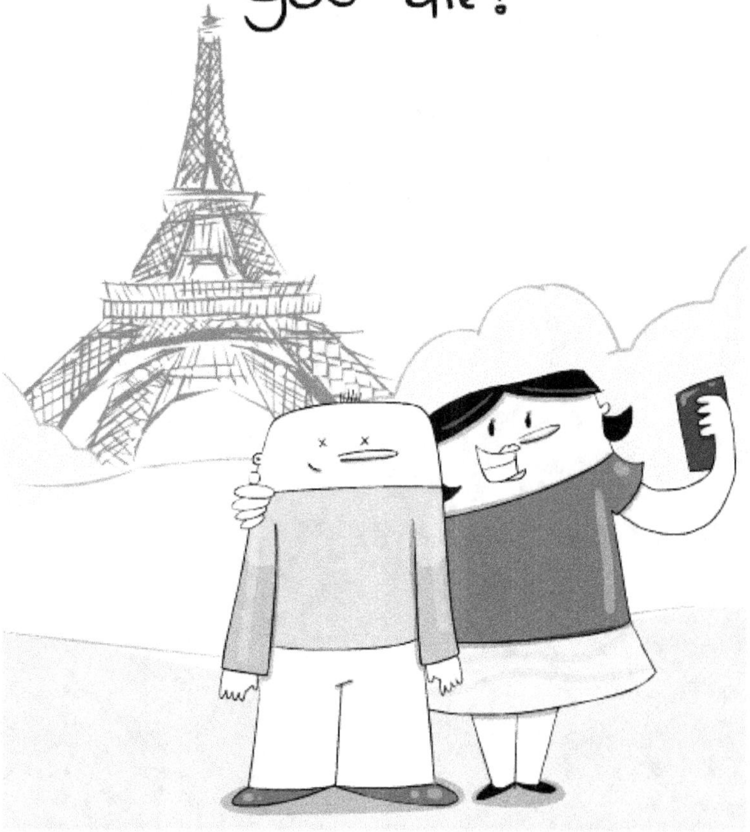

92.

To star in the 17th reboot of Spiderman because why not?

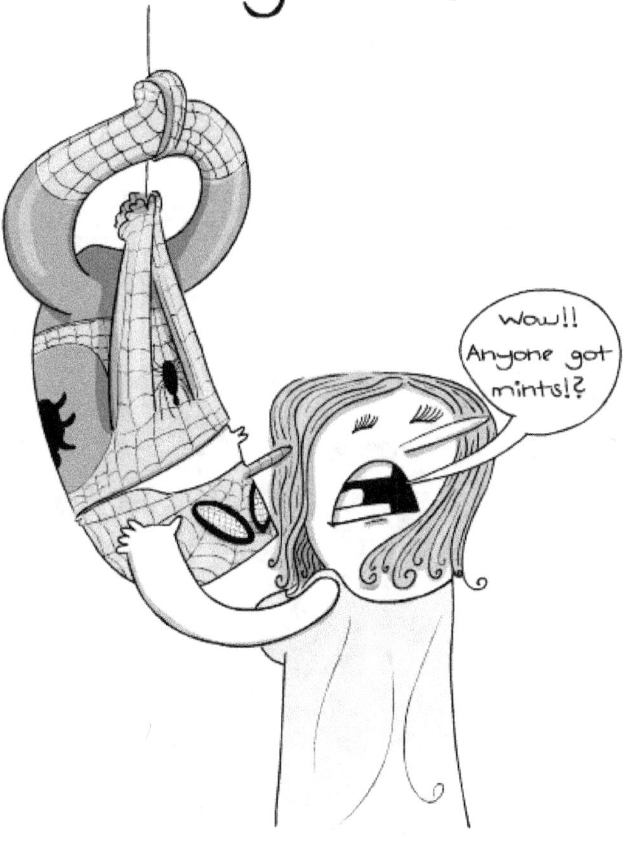
Wow!! Anyone got mints!?

93.

To talk to your kids about safe sex before it's too late. Because you won't.

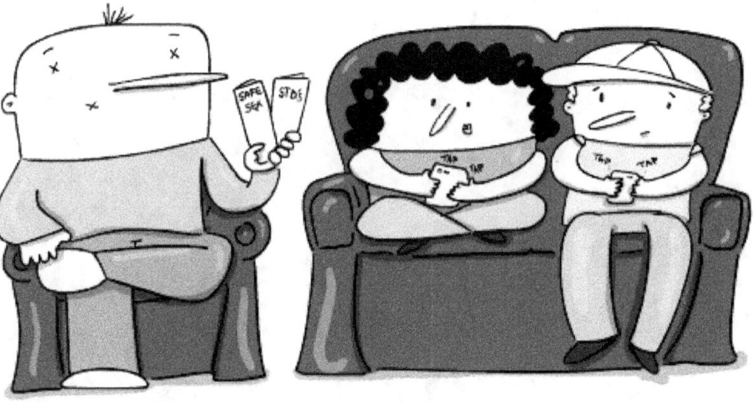
SAFE SEX
STDs

94.

your social media picture because hey, no one's picture is real anyway.

95.

A liver donor because you know you drink more than you should.

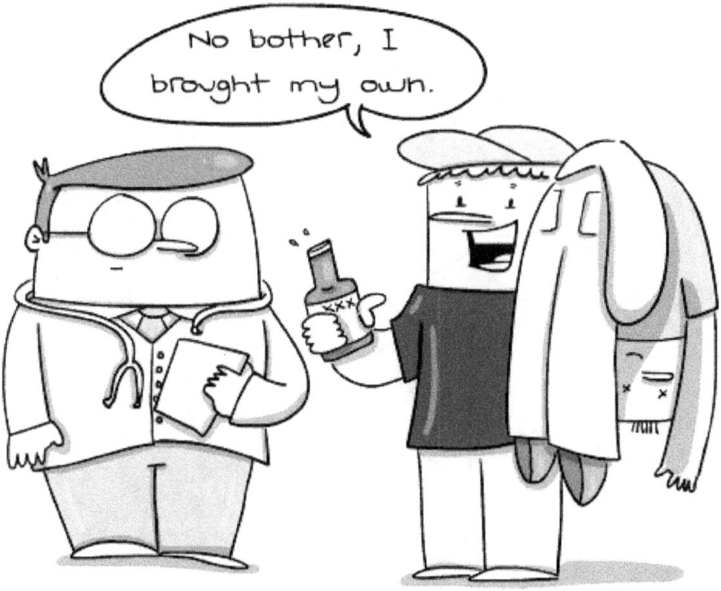
No bother, I brought my own.

96.

friend with benefits.

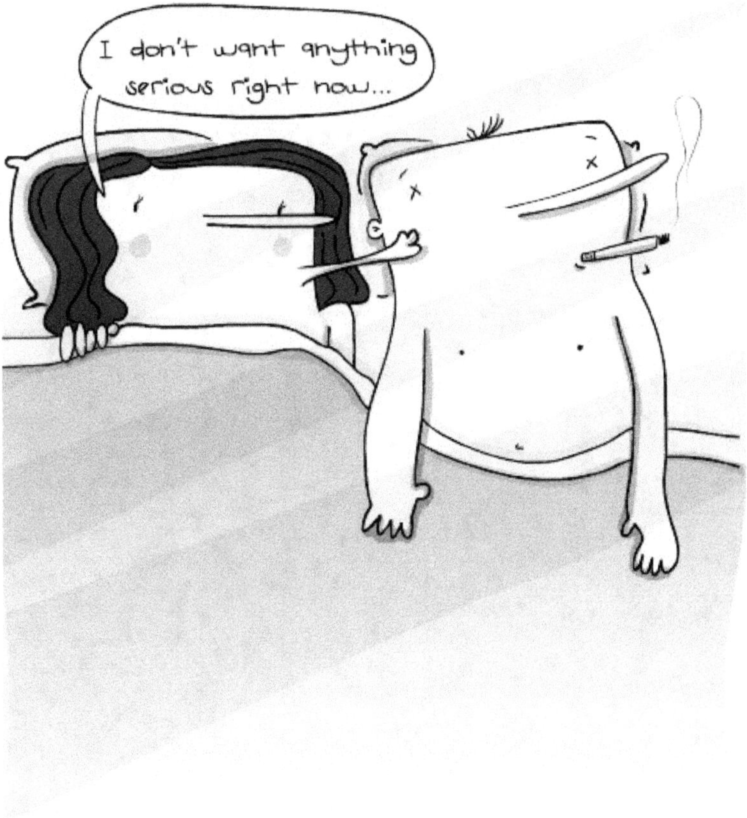
I don't want anything serious right now...

મ 97.

To spend quality time with your family because you're too busy at work.

98.

Imagine it has a better life than you and hate yourself for it.

99.

A constant reminder that you will die and be forgotten like everyone else.

100.

A constant reminder that your life could end at any minute and you're wasting it.

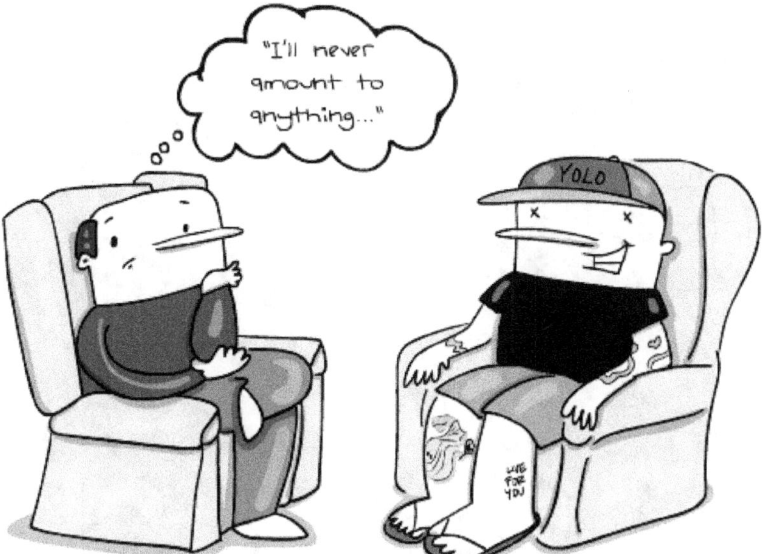
"I'll never amount to anything..."
YOLO

101.

To remind you that your life could end at any minute so live each moment to the fullest!.

"To be continued..."

EMILY CAESAR is a Los Angeles based animator and cartoonist. Her videos and artwork are about illustrating different ideas while making people smile, laugh, and think. Emily can be found at her websites: Animationstation.com and EmilyCartoons.com.

JASON BLAKE was raised in the swamp of rural Georgia. An expat from the continental US, Jason hides on a remote tropical island. On the rare occasions when his Netflix queue is empty, Jason contemplates the big ideas that can move humanity forward together like better box wine and spreadable cheese technology.

Contributors

Peggy Geary Rubenstein
Ross Martineau
Philip Steinbacher
Larraine Castillo Woods
Cherie Pipkin
Ricky March
Michelle Blake
Suzanna Kennedy
Chuck Lasker
Edwin Sawyer
Tim Sample
Melissa Steinbacher Wood
Mary Greco
Kenneth Florence
Nathan Rubenstein
Rowdy Morris
Gwen Margolis
Faith Harding
Melissa Egusa

www.ingramcontent.com/pod-product-compliance
Lightning Source LLC
Chambersburg PA
CBHW070733020526
44118CB00035B/1272